Don't You Know
Who I Am?

35 Years of Being Ignored by Sport's Rich and Famous

Peter Slater

To Mervyn
Best wishes
Peter Slater.

Vertical Editions

www.verticaleditions.com

First published in the United Kingdom in 2013 by Vertical Editions, Unit 4a, Snaygill Industrial Estate, Skipton, North Yorkshire BD23 2QR

www.verticaleditions.com

ISBN 978-1-904091-74-5

A CIP catalogue record for this book is available from the British Library

Cover design by HBA, York

Printed and bound by CMP, Dorset

For Alison, who does know who I am

Contents

Harry Redknapp's Mobile Phone (Life in the Tunnel)   7

Prologue: In the Beginning   10

1   Damon Hill Hit Me   16

2   Muhammad Ali and the American Hitch-Hiker   26

3   On Being Drunk In Charge of a Steve Davis Interview   31

4   Brian Clough and the Handsome Young Man   37

5   Geoffrey Boycott and the Blonde Bombshell   41

6   Bobby Robson … Without Whom   45

7   Fergie, His Rants in My Earhole   53

8   Driving the Back Roads of France with Mika Hakkinen   59

9   Ross Brawn and the Football Dinner   64

10   Gary Lineker's Sitting on the Edge of My Bed   71

11   Doing the Poznan, Sir Chris Hoy and the Berlin to
     Warsaw Express   76

12   Wembley – Venue of Embarrassment and Humiliation   88

13   Eric Cantona Says "Oui", Steve Bruce Says "No"   93

14   Who's That Behind Martin Brundle?   97

15   F***ing Brilliant … the Perils of the Football League
     Play-Offs   103

16   Bill Shankly is Surprised   111

17   North-East Enders (the Newcastle United Soap Opera)   115

18   A Weekend at Gleneagles with Mark Knopfler,
     Captain Mark Phillips and Jackie Stewart   149

19 If We Put the Microphone Next to the Air Conditioner it Might Just Sound Like a Helicopter (Faking It on the Tour de France)   157

20 "And Jimmy Glass Has Scored for Carlisle United!"   173

21 Slightly Sideways – Motor Bikes with No Brakes   180

22 Woke Up, Had Breakfast, Interviewed Dull Scot (Colin McRae and the World Rally Championship)   186

23 Flying Down to Rio … What Happened Next   192

24 A-Z – An Alphabetical List of Others I Have Met   199

Harry Redknapp's Mobile Phone (Life in the Tunnel)

I was standing next to Harry Redknapp in the tunnel at Molineux the other day. Spurs had beaten Wolves and there he was with a pair of headphones on waiting for our presenter Mark Pougatch to interview him on *Sports Report*. I was wearing a second pair of headphones so I could act as the link between the studio and the interviewee. It's standard practice in my strange world, where the routine in that hour after the final whistle blows is now reasonably set in stone.

At around three-quarter time at whichever match I'm reporting from, the editor of the day will come on the line for a chat. This is usually to say that they'd like me to broadcast my match report "live" from the tunnel and then try and find us an interview for the show. With more than 2.5 million listeners, *Sport on 5* and *Sports Report* are still major players on a Saturday afternoon and the football world respects that.

It still makes for a fraught 30 minutes or so as you have to de-rig all your wires and boxes, pack them up, cart them down to the interview point, set everything up again and re-dial, all the time rehearsing what your final report is going to say. Ideally you should have it all about written on the final whistle, but late equalisers and winners mean that's not always possible.

Anyway, back to Harry, always just about the most amenable manager after the game. There was a slight delay as Pougatch was already in the middle of another interview. Mark Williams the producer had come on the line to apologise and promise Harry we'd be with him within the next 60 seconds. Harry said that wasn't a problem and put his hand into his pocket and brought out his mobile phone.

Now you'd expect someone like Redknapp to have the latest of gadgets, maybe even more than one, but instead he revealed an ancient instrument, even older than the one I'd traded in several years before. I said to him that it looked pretty old and he quipped back, "Yeah, it's an antique, just like me."

He didn't have time to text anyone before Pougatch was ready to do the interview. Harry answered the questions, said goodbye and moved on to his next commitment. It was as easy as that. This is live broadcasting in the second decade of the 21st century. You meet, you chat and you go your separate ways.

Down in the tunnel post-match is about as close to the coal face of the business as it's possible to be nowadays. Years ago though you were lucky to be allowed anywhere near. I remember negotiating with Ipswich Town for ages to be allowed to stand inside the door to the dressing room corridor so I could record interviews with the players once the match had finished. Many years later when I returned to Ipswich, BBC Radio had an ISDN interview point installed in the very room where I used to take my victims and, of course, I was allowed in. Things had moved on.

Nowadays all the top clubs have an army of press officers to smooth the way between five o'clock and 5.45, when the media needs to do its stuff. If you have the right pass then you're in, and the BBC, who pay a lot of money for the privilege, make sure I always do have the right pass. There are TV rooms with the sponsor's boards, so that no-one is ever spoken to without the advertising behind them. Sometimes there are radio rooms, where managers and players arrive, and it's then all about timing. If it works well then *Sports Report* features all the top names live, sometimes with hilarious results.

One winter Saturday evening at Sunderland's Stadium of Light, their then manager Steve Bruce had promised to talk to us, except that he arrived just as Pougatch cued me in. Steve saw what was happening and took the extra set of headphones from my outstretched hand. It was a reporter's nightmare since I had to give the nation my opinion on what had happened with the manager listening in. It actually made great radio because, as I finished, I was able to say to Mark, "That's my view of the game and I hope Steve Bruce agrees because he's heard every word." Cue laughter all round and an excellent piece of radio concluded by the Sunderland manager talking to us live.

Welcome to the modern day sports reporter's world. A world of pooled press conferences and players protected by their own clubs' media departments, a world where you can be treated like a king one day and like dirt the next. A world where you have status which allows you into places the normal punter would never go, but no status at all in the great scheme of things. You are a conduit and, as Marshall McLuhan once said, "The medium is the message", all you're doing is delivering it. Sometimes, like with Steve Bruce or Harry Redknapp, it works, on other occasions it doesn't.

I've been delivering the message for over 35 years, pretty much all my working life. I've been pushed around, sworn at, assaulted; I've been frozen in press boxes, broiled in pit lanes, drenched so much once that my shoes disintegrated and yet I've loved every minute of it. The job has taken me around the world several times including to places you'd never normally go.

I've interviewed just about everyone there is to interview in football over the decades and plenty of other sports people as well. Along the way the odd rock star, politician and celebrity chef have faced my microphone but the meetings are always fleeting, we walk in, we talk and we go home. I remember them but I doubt very much if they remember me but that's just the way it is. So let me share with you just a few of the things which have happened to me and are still happening. Harry Redknapp, meanwhile, has promised to upgrade his mobile.

Prologue: In the Beginning

I think I always wanted to be the man who came on after the football results and talked about the game.

As a child, whilst others had more obvious heroes: Bobby Charlton and George Best, Ted Dexter and Colin Cowdrey, Jim Clark and Graham Hill, the people I looked up to were those telling me about these sporting giants.

I remember going to a Scout camp one summer in the early 1960s and being bored to tears. The only thing which kept me sane was listening to England racking up a massive first innings score in the Old Trafford Test Match against Australia. I can still remember, without reference to any search engine, that Dexter scored 174 and Ken Barrington 256. Most of all I recall John Arlott, the finest broadcaster of his or any other generation, calmly describing the scene as I huddled in a tent in North Yorkshire just longing to go home.

In the winter, when the cricketers went on tour, occasionally you could pick up very crackly reports from far, far away. At home, Bill Bothwell, Larry Canning and Bryon Butler were the people to listen to. Bothwell reported from the north, so he was usually at Old Trafford or Goodison Park. Larry Canning covered the Midlands; Aston Villa and Wolverhampton Wanderers were his teams, BB was in London, where Arsenal, Chelsea and the great double winning Tottenham Hotspur dominated. Later in my life I would employ Larry Canning and work alongside Bryon, I'd also interview Bill Nicholson and members of that Spurs team, but back then it was my early contact with football, the game that I loved.

It was a geography lesson as well, as these masters of the

airwaves appeared one week in Burnley, the next in Stoke, or down on the south coast with Southampton and Portsmouth. I learnt much about who came from where, and even then I'm sure I was thinking that if I couldn't play the game to a high level, which was already unlikely, then the next best thing would be telling others about it whilst travelling up and down the country in the process.

At school, where English turned out to be my best subject, I used to take part in the public speaking competitions and I usually won them. In the school play I was given good parts and even joined the County Youth Theatre. I watched football when I could, first at Ayresome Park in Middlesbrough, then St. James' Park when my father changed jobs and we moved to Newcastle. My heroes were John Hickton, a right back converted to a goal scoring inside forward, and "Jinky" Jimmy Smith, a midfielder who could enthral and frustrate in equal measure, depending what head he had on in any particular game. He was my kind of player. At Sheffield University it was Hillsborough one week, Bramall Lane the next when Tony Currie delighted and when I would also write match reports for my hall newsletter under the pen name of V. Boring. I was editing the paper and making programmes for the student radio group, ironically called Radio 5, and so by the time I graduated in the summer of 1974 I had experience of writing, editing and broadcasting.

A year later I was back in Newcastle, having done some travelling (it's called a Gap Year nowadays, then it was just avoiding joining the rat race for as long as possible) and deciding what to do with my life. I wanted to join the BBC but the only way in was the station assistants register, which put you on a waiting list for consideration when jobs arose on BBC local radio stations. I duly applied and also wrote to the local hospital radio station. After that there was nothing left for it but to sit back and wait.

To earn some money I found a job selling advertising on the *Newcastle Evening Chronicle*. I was quite good to be honest, travelling the east of the city and working with motor dealers, but my heart was never in it. I did some writing and Sylvia Horn at BBC Radio Newcastle bought a couple of my scripts, but as the winter of 1976 turned into spring I was still travelling around in my sales reps Ford Escort, waiting for something to happen. Then in May it did, and how!

Over the course of one weekend I received two letters. One was from the BBC, inviting me to an interview for the aforementioned station assistants register. The other was from Radio Tyneside, Newcastle's hospital radio station, which was holding auditions. The same weekend I was also offered a flat which I'd been interested in for some time. It was all starting to come together but I couldn't have imagined just how quickly things would change.

On Saturday May 22^{nd,} after I'd been for an interview in Leeds, the BBC sent a letter accepting me onto the SA's register. Two days later I went along to the Radio Tyneside audition where all I had to do was give my name and address, out loud, in a room full of other hopefuls. At the end of this strange process, the station manager thanked everyone for attending but said he was sorry they wouldn't be taking them on as prospective broadcasters, "All except you," and he pointed at me. I was in, just like that.

The following Saturday, Radio Tyneside invited me in to help with their sports progamme. I wasn't there to broadcast, but within half an hour I was on the air putting some flesh on the bones of the afternoons' football scores as the season drew to a close. Two days later, with my new press card tucked inside my pocket, I went to the Newcastle City Hall and interviewed George Melly and Humphrey Lyttleton. I was completely intoxicated, mainly due to the fact that my card allowed me to stand at the back of the City Hall and listen to the concerts. A week later I was offered my own programme.

It was a Thursday night and I took to it like a duck to water. All I had to do was spin a few discs, talk in between and re-hash the news headlines which were given to me by a studio assistant who'd lifted them from the *Evening Chronicle*. As spring turned to summer my life had suddenly improved one hundred per cent. What followed was to make all that seem like very small beer indeed.

At the end of June, in the middle of the Wimbledon fortnight with temperatures continuing to soar as the long, hot summer of 1976 continued, I went into work on a Monday morning. My first port of call was Minories, one of the top motor dealers in the city. Their advertising manager was Paula Bell, and she was about to change my life forever. The conversation went something like this.

PAULA: "I've been away helping out on an ITV golf tournament this weekend, along with Charles Harrison. Do you know who Charles is?

ME: "I've heard the name"

PAULA: "He's the sports editor of Metro Radio (the new commercial radio station in Newcastle).

ME: "Ah yes, I've been down to speak to them about possible jobs."

I had indeed caught the bus down to their studios back in 1974, when they'd just started broadcasting. I'd spoken to one of their producers, who'd promised to keep me informed of any suitable vacancies. He hadn't, mainly because, although I didn't know this, he'd been fired when Metro realised that they didn't need producers on commercial radio.

PAULA: "Now you do hospital radio, and you're interested in sport, and I can tell you don't like this job very much."

ME: "You're probably right there."

PAULA, "Charles is looking for an assistant and he can't find anyone suitable. Would you be interested?"

Now St Paul had his vision on the road to Damascus, and I had my vision in the east end of Newcastle on that Monday morning.

ME: "Of course I'd be interested."

PAULA: "OK, I'll call him. "

So she did, right there in her office, and told Charles that she had a young man alongside her who she though he should speak to. Not only that, she handed the phone to me and I nervously found myself speaking to the sports editor of Metro

Radio.

I told him what I'd done, that I could edit and operate the technical equipment, and that I was a big sports fan. We arranged to meet that night in a pub called The Wheatsheaf in the east end of the city. Charles and I chatted, and we seemed to get on, especially when I bought him a beer. He asked me to come down for an audition the following morning and so on Tuesday, instead of cold calling in the wilds of Northumberland, I was sitting in the Metro Radio studio in Swalwell reading the racing results, conducting a mock interview with Charles, who was pretending to be Malcolm Macdonald, and giving my views on the possible winner of the Women's Singles at Wimbledon. Watching on was Mic Johnson, the Programme Controller, who then interviewed me in his office, asking me about my experience of radio.

Looking back, I was in exactly the right place at exactly the right time. If I could have engineered a particular job to fit my qualifications and interests, then this would have been it.

Charles and I parted with him telling me he'd give me an answer within 72 hours. On Wednesday I saw Paula again. She told me that Charles had told her what he thought of my audition, but that she could say no more. Charles had gone away for a couple of days.

On Friday morning, with my nerves stretched to breaking point, there was a phone call in the sales reps office at the *Evening Chronicle*. It was for me and it was a Mr Harrison. He asked me to come down to the station at lunchtime to meet the managing director, Neil Robinson.

Neil asked me a lot about my career ambitions, as well as my university education, and we shook hands at the end of the interview with me still in the dark about whether I'd got the job or not. Charles then took me up to the News Room to meet news editor Kevin Rowntree.

CHARLES: "Kevin, this is Peter, who's going to be joining the Sports Department."

I could hardly believe it. This was the first I'd heard about it, but in that room I could see editing machines and spools of tape, and through the glass was Studio One, on the air and broadcasting to the North-East. It seemed like home.

On my way out of the building I mentioned to Charles that so far I hadn't been offered a job. He assured me that I would be, and as I left Swalwell I was in a daze. In five short days my whole life had been turned around forever, and I mean forever.

Sure enough, within a few days a formal offer arrived. It was for a six month probationary contract, on less money than I was earning at the *Evening Chronicle*. There were no bonuses, no company car, no guarantee that come Christmas I'd still be in a job. I couldn't sign the forms quickly enough.

That was a long, long time ago and it proved to be the right decision. Just before Christmas in 1976 I was given a full-time post and my salary was increased by 30 per cent. After four and a half years at Metro I moved onto Radio Orwell in Ipswich and then down to London and the lure of the BBC Sports Unit, which remains the best in the world. Since 1989 I've been back in the north, working as their man in the region, with the added bonus of eight years in Formula One, a spot of World Rallying, and latterly the Tour de France. In March 2012 I left the corporation and now work as a freelance broadcaster, still doing shifts for them when asked. I've been fortunate enough to interview the great and the good, but if Paula Bell hadn't gone on a golf tournament and Charles Harrison hadn't been looking for an assistant then my life would have been very different.

1

Damon Hill Hit Me

Damon Hill's blow landed straight into the right hand side of my rib cage. By the time I realised exactly what had happened, the former World Motor Racing Champion had turned on his heels and disappeared into the safety of his Jordan team's motorhome. I had this dull pain in my chest and the sense that I had been struck, but the media scrum which surrounds F1 drivers is never the most serene of places, and for all I knew Kai Ebel from RTL television may have been the one to have inflicted the pain. Kai was renowned in boxing circles in Germany and it was his home Grand Prix after all. He and I hadn't been seeing eye to eye since I managed to interview David Coulthard when he thought it was his turn. Maybe he'd just barged me out of the way as he looked for the first reaction interview, the one we all want.

On this occasion, on an August afternoon in the middle of the Hockenheim paddock, Kai was innocent. The strike had been landed by Hill, and an F1 Digital TV crew had captured it on film. Within the hour it was the talk of the media centre, that giant tent at one end of the paddock where the bouncy floor made editing very difficult. Journalists from Japanese magazines were wanting to speak to me, the Jordan team press officer, Giselle Davies, couldn't believe what had happened, Damon had headed for the airport.

So why had Hill, normally so polite and accommodating, suddenly lashed out at a BBC Radio reporter with whom he'd previously enjoyed a cordial and, so I thought, mutually supportive relationship? After all I'd been interviewing him on a regular basis for nearly three years, since I'd started covering

F1 in 1997, when he was defending his title and driving for Tom Walkinshaw's Arrows team.

The Paddock gossip suggested that Hill had lost his bottle, and that he no longer wanted to risk his life driving fast cars around the circuits of the world. After all he was retiring at the end of the season and in Germany that afternoon it was alleged that he'd simply parked his car when there was nothing wrong with it. Later on Hill was to say that he'd had problems with the brakes and that he'd nearly collided with the Austrian driver Alexander Wurz. The Jordan team, and most of the press corps, didn't share his view.

Historically of course, Damon Hill had every right to be concerned about safety in F1. His father had been a driver and was killed in a plane crash returning from a test session. He was a test driver at Williams and was given his chance of the big time when Ayrton Senna was killed at Imola in 1994. He had been denied the crown by Michael Schumacher in 1995, but had become champion in Japan the following year. It was an emotional moment, captured superbly by Murray Walker on BBC TV. Then having failed to agree financial terms with Frank Williams for the 1997 campaign Hill had taken the strange step of signing for Arrows, a team who were never going to be competitive.

What he didn't know when he won the title was that by the time he arrived in Melbourne in March of that year, he'd be coming face to face with Radio 5 Live's new pit lane reporter. Mind, when he won that title I had no idea that I'd be the man saddled with the job of asking him to explain yet another poor qualifying session or mechanical failure throughout the 1997 campaign.

One Friday afternoon in late October of 1996, my mobile rang as I was standing outside a gents outfitters in Bakewell. I can't explain exactly what I was doing there, but I remember the call almost word for word.

It came from Gordon Turnbull, Editor of Radio Sport. It went something like this;

GT: "Peter, you know you've just been made a full-time

broadcaster, (Bob Shennan, the Head of Sport, had confirmed it the previous week). Well Iain Carter's decided he doesn't want to be our Formula One pit lane reporter anymore, and I wondered if you'd like to do it?"

ME: "Of course I would. Next question."

So Gordon went on to explain that Simon Taylor, who was our F1 commentator, needed someone who could go out to races on a Thursday, cover the press conferences and do the voice pieces until he arrived on Friday night. Simon would then do the commentary, and I'd have to stay over until Monday morning to sweep up any stories which had developed after the race.

This was just what I'd joined the BBC for, to do a spot of travelling whilst covering sport.

ME: "I assume that you want me to start when the European season kicks in then?"

GT: "No, Damon Hill's World Champion, so we want you in Australia and South America."

The first three races were Melbourne, Sao Paolo and Buenos Aires, so you can imagine my feelings that afternoon. I had to sit down on the stone window sill of the shop to gather myself. After 20 years in the business I'd been handed a dream job.

The following week Simon Taylor resigned. He'd been offered a job on ITV, who'd just secured the TV rights to cover F1. That job lasted a year incidentally. BBC Radio decided to appoint a motor racing correspondent to replace Simon, so when I touched down in Melbourne the following spring, I was part of a new team. There was me and Jonathan Legard. As we sat and enjoyed lunch overlooking Port Philip Bay on our first day in Australia, little did we know we'd be together for eight seasons.

Meanwhile in the temporary garages across town in Albert Park, Tom Walkinshaw's mechanics were preparing the car for Damon Hill to begin his title defence.

Now I need to mention at this stage that I'd already interviewed Damon Hill. That was when he'd driven for Brabham at Silverstone back in 1992. I'd found him to be polite, articulate and co-operative. To be fair he needed the publicity and we'd been happy to give it to him. By the time we met again in Australia in the week leading up to the first race of the new season, I'm sure he hadn't remembered that. Still, he'd been his usual self in the build-up to the race, and as the gentlemen started their engines, Jonathan in the commentary box and myself behind the pit garages waited for the action to begin.

I'd done the odd bit of pit work before, but only as a producer. Once, at Silverstone, Garry Richardson and I had been on the pit wall when Ayrton Senna broke down right in front of us. As Senna took off his helmet, I put a pair of headphones on him and Garry actually interviewed him, probably before the poor chap knew what was happening. That, as it turned out, was at the root of Damon's Hockenheim attack, but I'll come back to that.

Now I was the main man. If anything happened then I had to report it. I hoped for a quiet afternoon to bed myself in. It should be pointed out here that Damon Hill was always one of motor racing's gentlemen. There were certain drivers who liked to party, even during a race weekend, but he wasn't one of them. One driver I knew liked to have beauty queens brought in for him to enjoy, and another driver was actually encouraged by his team to go and find a woman the night before a race because, to quote one of the management: "He drives better with his saddlebags empty!"

The drivers lined up on the grid and went off on their installation lap. This is the one they do as the grid is cleared of mechanics and hangers on. Halfway round Damon Hill's Arrows car stopped. He just pulled it off the track and stopped. The rest of the cars continued to the start, and as the red lights went out they headed for the first corner, where Johnny Herbert and Eddie Irvine had a coming together and both spun out of the race. In these early days I didn't have a radio microphone, so any interviews had to be recorded. I then had to race up to the media centre and feed them in from our ISDN point at the back of the room.

When they retire from the race the drivers are usually returned to the paddock on the back of a motor bike or else they just walk there. There are only a couple of entrances and the media pack, those radio and TV crews who are on hand to bring instant reaction to their audiences at home, know pretty well where they'll find their prey. That afternoon Damon was the first to return, clutching his helmet and looking a tad sheepish as one might expect. His press officer at Arrows was Anne Bradshaw, one of the best in the business, who'd followed him from Williams. She knew the media would want to speak to him immediately, and the pecking order was ITV first, then ourselves.

Louise Goodman, herself a former press officer, now, like me, covering her first race as a pit lane reporter for ITV, stopped Damon and Annie.

LOUISE: "Damon, what happened?"

Damon gave a short answer and waited for the follow up question. It never came. Louise said thank you and handed back to Murray Walker. Damon looked at me as if to say, "Is that it?" and I steamed in to find out why he'd stopped, what his feelings were and if there'd been any indication before the race of problems etc. It was a much better interview, although I say so myself. Louise had just been overcome with first day nerves, and we later became good friends, often working together as a British team against the rest of the world, especially Kai Ebel and the Germans.

At that moment Messrs Herbert and Irvine arrived, not exactly pleased with each other. For a moment you wondered if a fight was going to break out, after all Eddie was never backward in coming forward and Johnny always had a thing or two to say for himself. So not a particularly quiet day for the Brits then. Oh, and David Coulthard went on to win. It wasn't always like that.

So Damon and I were off and running. The Arrows car wasn't very good, but after every practice and qualifying session, I'd be there at the back of the garage to speak to the man some of my colleagues had christened "The Mushroom" (it's all about champignon being like champion, you must forgive them). By mid-season I was sometimes the only person interested in speaking to Hill, and Ann Bradshaw was always pleased to see me. I think Damon was too.

In August, at the Hungarian Grand Prix, the Arrows car showed signs of improvement. They managed to qualify third and on the Saturday night, at the inaugural FOFIFO dinner, organised for Fans of Football in Formula One, (covered at greater length elsewhere) there was much talk about whether Damon Hill could actually win the race. We then proceeded to stand on the chairs of a very posh Budapest restaurant singing the tune to *Match of the Day* as the Hungarian Gypsy Band played along. It was just another typical F1 Saturday really.

The Sunday was baking hot. It always was in Budapest. Thousands of Finns were in town to watch Mika Hakkinen, and Williams were looking to Jacques Villeneuve to take another victory on the way to winning the World Title. Down in the Arrows garage, Nigel Green, one of their marketing men and someone who became a good friend during his time in F1, was confidently showing clients around the garage. As the race started, Hill accelerated into the lead. Nigel grew ever more excited, but being British was convinced it couldn't last. However Damon wasn't going to hand over his advantage, and as the race entered its final stages, he was still in front of Villeneuve, and Arrows were on course for their first ever F1 victory.

Wanting to be part of history, Louise and I gathered at the back of the garage. Nigel was looking agitated. What he knew and we didn't was that Damon's car had an electrical problem and was about to lose the lead. Nigel gave us the bad news, but I could do nothing with the information. Remember that I had no radio microphone, and so as Jonathan Legard and co-commentator Maurice Hamilton were in celebratory mood across the track, I knew the truth, but had no way of telling either them or the listeners what was about to happen. By the time I'd raced back to the media centre to let them know, it already had. The luckless Hill was passed by Villeneuve, and we had to conduct a bitter sweet interview on the stairs of the media centre, as Damon told me about the misery of finishing second. Through it all, though, he behaved like a gentleman, which made the events in Hockenheim even more of a surprise.

Hill's association with Arrows was already coming to an end by the time the F1 circus moved on from Hungary. When we reached Austria in September the rumour became truth. Damon Hill had signed a two year deal to drive for Eddie Jordan. It was a real coup for the ebullient Irishman and gave Hill a much stronger team to work with. EJ, as everyone knew Eddie, was like the cat who'd stolen the cream on the Friday morning when the announcement was made official, and he even gave BBC Radio an interview ahead of the press conference, so we could run it in the *Today* programme on Radio 4. That's how important the news was.

I think overall Hill and Jordan were good for each other. He even gained them their first Grand Prix victory in Belgium in 1998, the most eventful race I ever covered, when Michael Schumacher threatened to kill David Coulthard and I ended up interviewing a very emotional EJ next to the rubbish bins in Spa. It's all glamour you know.

That was also the year when Damon made my son's day. Damon was Stephen's big hero, and so I arranged for Steve to spend the day with me at the Monaco Grand Prix. It was the day when there was no racing, and the family were on holiday just down the coast, so one very excited 11 year-old found himself in the paddock, where he had lunch with Murray Walker and met so many famous people he didn't quite know whose autograph to ask for next. But he'd not met his number one idol and I had a special plan to make this happen.

In the evening, as Stephen was beginning to fray a little bit around the edges, I took him down to where the team trucks were. I knew that inside one of them Damon Hill was meeting with his mechanics, planning strategy for the following days qualifying. Now part of the job of any reporter is "hanging around". We're used to it, sometimes having to wait hours for the appearance of our prospective interviewee, who often declines to say anything to us anyway.

So we waited and waited, until out of the truck came … Gary Anderson. Stephen didn't know who Gary was, but I did, and it meant that before long the moment we'd been waiting for would arrive. Gary was EJ's chief engineer, a quiet, thoughtful Ulsterman, excellent company and another F1 gentleman.

"Waiting for our new truckie are you?" he said to me, assessing the situation perfectly. "He won't be long." Stephen didn't understand what he meant, but sure enough a few moments later out came Damon. As he saw the obvious father son combination he came over to Stephen.

DH: "This your Dad?"

STEPHEN: A nod of the head (he was too tongue tied to say anything).

DH: "Causes me nothing but trouble, always asking questions."

And in the days before iPhones and a lot of digital technology, where everyone wants to be seen with famous people, Damon Hill shook hands with Stephen and posed for a photograph. I had it developed and enlarged, mounted but not framed. I then took it back for Damon to sign and had the glass and frame added. It remains one of my son's most treasured possessions.

All of which makes what occurred that afternoon in Germany even more inexplicable. Here was a top sportsman with whom I'd had a good relationship. I wouldn't say we were close, that never happens, but he was the last person I'd have expected to hit me.

To put things into sharper context, when Damon Hill arrived in Germany in early August 1999 we already knew that he was going to quit at the end of the season. He'd admitted as much to me in an emotional interview at the French Grand Prix in Magny Cours back in June.

After the race in Hockenheim, a race won by Eddie Irvine for Ferrari by the way, we found ourselves back in Budapest. On the Thursday afternoon Giselle Davies came looking for me. Giselle was one of the best press officers in the paddock, she's the daughter of Barry Davies, one of BBC TV's legendary commentators, and fluent in pretty well every language you could hope to name. She told me that Damon had asked to see me, and would I please come to the Jordan Motorhome, and bring my recording equipment with me.

When I arrived, Giselle ushered me into the air conditioned bus, and there was Damon. She left us alone. What followed was one of the most humbling experiences of my reporting life. Damon Hill, one time World Motor Racing Champion, BBC Sports Personality of the Year and all round good guy, wanted to apologise to me.

I'm not going to pass on here all of what was said in the room, some of it was off the record and a reporter never breaks that sort of confidence if he wants to survive in the business. However, one thing Damon did say, which I can repeat, explains better than anything else the relationship between sportsman and interviewer at that "interface" moment.

Damon admitted that he'd elbowed me in the ribs. He told me that when you get out of the car it's like you've just been in a fight and the last thing you want to do is speak to anyone, let alone a bunch of quote hungry journalists who are probably just out to have a go at you. So he attacked the first thing he came into contact with, and that just happened to be my ribcage.

I told him that I understood his point of view. I explained that I was only doing my job and that I'd have been failing in my duty if I hadn't been there to speak to him. We parted on good terms, and he'd even given me an exclusive interview, re-affirming his commitment to the Jordan cause for the rest of the season.

Which was exactly what he gave. Even in the cramped team quarters in Suzuka after his final race, Damon was gracious enough to grant me one last interview. He remains one of my favourite interviewees, and that framed photo is still on my son's bedroom wall, the starry eyed 11 year old with his hero, a moment captured forever.

I joke that I can still feel the pain where the elbow of Damon

Hill "interfaced" with my ribs. It's an incident which lasted a split second, a moment when the sportsman loses that self-discipline which keeps him at the top of his game. On a scale of one to ten it's nowhere near Eric Cantona's kung fu kick, but it did happen, it must have happened, it was on YouTube for goodness sake.

So is that the only time I've been attacked during my work? Well a rather over enthusiastic club official did once push me over at Carrow Road as I was trying to interview Howard Kendall after Everton had won the title in 1987. If anything that annoyed me far more than Damon's indiscretion. At least Damon apologised, and gave me an exclusive interview.

2

Muhammad Ali and the American Hitch-Hiker

I've not come across many boxers in my radio career, but when I have the encounters have always been significant.

The first time I ever appeared on Radio 4 (a proud moment indeed) it was after I'd been sent to interview Barry McGuigan ahead of his World Title fight against Eusebio Pedroza. I once spoke to Nigel Benn in a hotel kitchen for reasons which now escape me, and the editor once asked me to produce a fight involving Herol "Bomber" Graham. Desmond Lynam did the commentary, Glenn McCrory was the summariser, but I can't even remember where it took place. All I do recall is Des complaining because the punters kept asking him where he'd been on holiday. At that time he was presenting the *Holiday Programme* on BBC TV, "and they think I spend all my time on vacation," he moaned. Mind you his sun tan was pretty impressive.

There was an occasion in the summer of 1977 when I was watching Virginia Wade winning Wimbledon on the only black and white TV on the first floor of Metro Radio and Henry Cooper wandered in. So we just sat there, me and the great man, watching Virginia overcoming Betty Stöve, as the crowd sang *For she's a Jolly Good Fellow*. I presumed that Henry had been in to do an interview on the afternoon programme, but he may just have driven all the way down to our studios in Swalwell simply to say that he was with me when Virginia triumphed, although I doubt it.

I did once watch Frank Bruno fight. He lost to James

"Bonecrusher" Smith at the Wembley Arena, but I was there to see the fight after Bruno's. It involved a bantamweight from Ipswich called Rory Burke, who was last on the bill. I was there to cover it for Radio Orwell, the Suffolk Radio Station where I was employed as sports editor. By the time Rory came into the ring, the hall was pretty well empty. The only pressmen still there, apart from the man from *Boxing News*, were me and Dave Allard from the *Ipswich Evening Star*. Rory lost by the way.

Oh, and I once interviewed Muhammad Ali.

Yes, that's correct, I once sat down next to the most famous sportsman of all time and asked him a few questions. It was just me and him on a sofa, not an organised press conference with dozens of cameras and sound recorders, not even the chaotic bun fight like when Brad Pitt, George Clooney and Matt Damon turned up at the Monaco Grand Prix and Radio One demanded a quote, any quote, from any one of the three superstars. That Saturday morning I did actually shout something to Clooney, like "George, what do you think of the cars?" and he shouted back, "They're great." Hardly incisive journalism, but *Newsbeat* seemed to like it.

However, in July 1977, at the Holiday Inn in Seaton Burn, half a dozen miles north of Newcastle upon Tyne, I was granted an exclusive audience with the Heavyweight Champion of the World.

So how did it happen that a callow youth still in his first year as a radio reporter was granted an interview which remains, more than 30 years on, the most memorable of my career? Well it was all down to a painter and decorator from Whitburn called Johnny Walker. Johnny ran a boxing club in South Shields, and he needed to raise money for it. Johnny had known Ali from his days involved in the sport, and so just called him up and asked if he would help. Astonishingly Ali said yes, and in the summer of the Queens Silver Jubilee he flew into the region.

That was some year for the North-East to be fair. Not only did we have Ali and Her Majesty in the region, but also the then

President of the United States, Jimmy Carter. Carter came to Newcastle and famously stood on the steps of the Civic Centre and said "Howay the lads." as the secret service men watched from the surrounding rooftops, guns pointed and ready. I was part of the Metro Radio team which covered all three events, but because I was primarily a sports reporter, when a call came through to the newsroom one warm afternoon, the news editor turned to me.

"Johnny Walker's just been on the phone, and Muhammad Ali will give the station an interview," he said. I think we'd been involved in some of the organisation of the trip, maybe we'd even helped sponsor it, I don't know. What I did know was that I immediately had to make my way across the city to the hotel where Ali and his entourage were staying. If I was lucky I'd be able to interview him. Was I nervous? You bet.

Security in the hotel was tight, not like if Jimmy Carter or The Queen were staying there, but a number of muscular looking gentlemen were hanging around in the foyer. However, when I arrived with my tape recorder, with Metro Radio emblazoned on the side, there was no problem. I was expected. I was ushered into a side room, and there, sitting on a sofa, was the man both he and everyone else called "The Greatest." Johnny Walker or one of his pals made the introductions and I was told that I had to keep things brief, which usually meant I'd be given around three minutes to complete the interview. No time for small talk then.

What I remember most of all was that there was an aura surrounding Ali. It's strange to mention it now, but it's stayed with me ever since. I've met many famous people in my career, but no-one else, not Michael Schumacher, Elton John, not even Pele (who I've interviewed twice incidentally) have had the same charisma. It was as if there was an invisible ring around him, protecting him from the rest of the world.

I still have the interview, it's on a tape reel in my loft. It lasted around three and a half minutes and I can remember almost everything in it, which is just as well because I no longer possess a machine on which to play it. I started by asking Ali about the North-East and his impressions of it, and then moved onto talking of his career, and what he was hoping to do next. He spoke about a possible upcoming fight, I think against Ken Norton, and also admitted that the punch which Henry Cooper floored him with back in the mid 1960s was "the hardest he'd ever received."

At the end of my time, with the minders making winding up movements, The Greatest finished the interview with his usual pay-off. "I like your show, I love your style, but your pay's so poor I won't be talking to you for a while."

I had it, the interview of my life. My job now was to deliver it safely back to the studios so we could scoop our rivals. Seaton Burn was six miles north of Newcastle, Swalwell was on the south side. To reach it I had to drive through the city and onto the Gateshead Western Bypass. I was driving the Metro Radio News Car, and as I swung onto the roundabout to take me south, I spotted a hitch-hiker. Having been one myself until only recently, I reckoned that I could do this guy a favour by giving him a lift through Newcastle and setting him on his way at a convenient roundabout on the south side. I stopped and wound down my window.

"I'm only going through the city," I told him, "but I can put you on the right road south if that's any good." He accepted my offer of a lift, put his rucksack on the back seat and joined me in the front of the car. He was American.

"So what do you do at the radio station?" he asked me, having seen the name plastered all over the car. "I'm a Sports Reporter," I replied, "and I've just been in that hotel interviewing Muhammad Ali."

My passenger gave me a look of incredulity. Either he didn't believe me or he thought me the biggest fantasist he'd ever had the misfortune to meet.

"Honestly," I said, "Ali's in town and I've just been in there talking to him." To confirm what I was telling him I asked him to reach onto the back seat and pass my tape recorder through. I sat it on his lap, rewound the tape and played him what I'd just recorded. I doubt his flabber had ever been more gasted.

There was The Greatest, laughing and joking and insulting the pecuniary capabilities of the radio station.

Soon we were through Newcastle and I had to let my bewildered passenger out of the car so he could go south and I could return to the studio. We broadcast the interview and my bosses were delighted. Later that week Ali even came into the studios and took part in a phone-in. The station used the photos of the event as part of their publicity campaigns for some time after that. They show Ali with his headphones under his chin rather than on his head, kind of upside down. No-one was going to tell him he'd got it wrong.

It's now several decades since he came to call, since he gave me that unforgettable interview. I'm older and greyer and when young people ask me, as they often do, who's the most famous person you've ever interviewed, the answer will always be "Muhammad Ali." They're still nearly always impressed.

It might be fanciful but I also like to think that somewhere in Middle America there's a middle aged man who'll be able to tell his children about the time he hitched a lift with a young, starry-eyed reporter who'd just conducted an interview with the most famous man in the world. "And he played me the interview to prove it. I actually had the tape recorder on my lap." he might tell them. It was all a long time ago, but, like me, I hope he's never forgotten the moment.

3

On Being Drunk In Charge of a Steve Davis Interview

When I worked in Ipswich, every February the town staged a snooker tournament. It was sponsored by the local brewery and went under the name of "The Tolly Cobbold Invitational". Anglia Television recorded some of it for broadcast later in the week and it provided Radio Orwell with plenty of material during an otherwise quiet time of year. Many of the Ipswich Town footballers were away on international duty, the Speedway season hadn't started and much of the local amateur sport was suffering at the hands of the weather. Tucked inside the warmth of the Corn Exchange, the town prepared to go "snooker loopy."

The event was promoted by Ted Brown, who ran a snooker hall in the middle of Ipswich. His job was to attract the top names in the sport to come and play, and back in those days snooker was big news, the players were major personalities, and to have them in Ipswich was great for everyone.

On the Friday before it all started, Ted arranged for me to record an interview with Dennis Taylor, the popular Ulsterman who was to win the World Title later in the decade. I was intrigued to find out that Dennis lived in Blackburn, but he provided me with some great material, which pleased Ted as well, since it gave his tournament extra publicity.

On the day before play began, some of the early arrivals went to Ted's house to play a few frames with those Ipswich Town players who weren't away representing their countries. I remember persuading the Ipswich goalkeeper Paul Cooper, himself a keen snooker player, to interview one time World Champion Cliff Thorburn. It made great radio.

Thorburn was one of the main draw cards. Others included Jimmy White, Tony Knowles, Alex "Hurricane" Higgins, and of course, Steve Davis. At that time Davis was the best player in the world. He'd been nurtured by Barry Hearn and was just about unbeatable. He also had a reputation for unspectacular play. Unlike Higgins or White, when Steve Davis came to the table, he was unlikely to leave it in a hurry.

When you're thrust into the close proximity of sportsmen for a while, you discover more about them than you ever could simply by watching on the TV. You learn which are the womanisers and the ones who like a drink, the ones who really appreciate their audience and those who treat them with arrogance and disdain. Into the latter category I'd immediately place Alex Higgins.

Now Higgins is no longer with us, his reputation has had something of a makeover. A brilliant documentary has explained how this fantastically gifted player from Belfast charmed the snooker world with his game, how he won the World Title but destroyed himself along the way, drinking and smoking himself to death.

I have one lasting image of Higgins, and it doesn't do him any favours. One night in the Ipswich Corn Exchange, a capacity crowd was eagerly waiting for him to come and play. He was late, and the audience, which included children, the sponsors who'd put the money in, and the TV crew who were waiting to broadcast the event, were growing impatient. For some reason I'd had to leave the building for a moment, and as I passed the pub which was next to the Exchange I looked through the window and there was Higgins, surrounded by his cronies, drinking and smoking without a care in the world as the audience were left to twiddle their collective thumbs. It may have been very rock and roll, but to me it seemed disrespectful to those who paid his wages. It soured my opinion of him, and that opinion wasn't helped by the fact that, out of all the players, Higgins was the only one who felt that speaking to the local radio station was beneath him.

Higgins didn't reach the final that year. The two players who did were Steve Davis and the genial Welshman Terry Griffiths. As they began their opening frame, the assembled media watched on the screen in the sponsors bar. Since it was the brewery who were putting up the cash the sponsors bar was quite definitely the place to be. They were serving champagne and we were drinking it.

The final started at around 7.30 in the evening and it was a close match, with neither player racing into a decisive lead. By midnight they were still going strong and the drink was still flowing. At around one o'clock in the morning Steve Davis prevailed, and was presented with the trophy by the Chairman of the brewery, Mr Patrick Cobbold, who was also the chairman of Ipswich Town.

By the time the ceremonials were completed it must have been close to two in the morning, and I then had to conduct an interview with the winner, despite having spent several hours availing myself of the sponsors finest products. Basically I was drunk.

I don't know if Steve realised this, maybe all snooker reporters suffered from spending too much time in the bar, but somehow we wrapped the interview successfully and I headed out into the cold Suffolk night.

From the Corn Exchange it was just a quick stagger up Lloyds Avenue and in through the back door of Electric House. The Radio Station was deserted at that time in the morning as I walked across to the network printer to see what material they'd sent. The system we operated was that the sports department would prepare a bulletin for the *Breakfast Show*, record it and leave it for the news producer to introduce at 08.30.

I was delighted to see that the England Football Team had beaten Turkey and that Ipswich's Terry Butcher had scored. That would make a good lead with Steve Davis taking the Tolly Cobbold a terrific second story. The bulletin would be a strong one.

So I wrote my script, edited the snooker interview and

recorded the piece for the following morning, feeling extremely pleased and confident. Then I went home and slept, until I awoke with that dull sensation which could only mean panic. Surely I couldn't have subjected the Radio Orwell listeners to a sports desk recorded under the influence of too much champagne? I looked at my watch and it was two minutes before the witching half hour that heralded what could become the most embarrassing moment of my career, the final moment of my career if my worst fears were realised.

It reminded me of an occasion in August 1977. Back then I was working in Newcastle for Metro Radio and we used to record a sports bulletin to be played into the *Night Owls* show, which was presented by James Whale. When there was midweek sport I'd work a late shift and do the bulletins live. If nothing was happening in the evening we'd simply re-hash the tea-time news, record it and leave it for James to play in. That night I'd gone out for a drink with my girlfriend and some other friends to a bar in Gosforth Park and as we drove home I switched on the car radio. They were playing an Elvis Presley track. When it finished James sounded sombre as he introduced the news bulletin, which was networked from London.

The newsreader also sounded downbeat. He started to read. "The world of music is tonight mourning Elvis Presley, who has died of a heart attack at the age of 42." The bulletin went on to chronicle the achievements of the great man before finishing with a network ident. Back came James, to say that he was sure all listeners would be saddened by the passing of Elvis, and that he'd be playing some more of his music, "After the Sports News with Peter Slater."

Then on came the most cheerful sounding sports desk you'd ever heard, completely out of synch with the mood of the evening. I sounded a right idiot, completely un-caring about the death of Elvis, who, of course, had been alive when I'd recorded it four hours earlier.

That hadn't been my fault. What was about to go out in Ipswich that morning was completely my doing. How could I have been so stupid? Why hadn't I just written a couple of cues and left it to the newsreader to cover me?

So I turned on the radio, but I turned it on very softly so that I could hardly hear it, assuming that if I couldn't hear it then neither could anyone else. The bulletin went out, the world didn't stop turning, and the programme controller didn't demand to see me in his office. In fact no-one said anything, which must say something about my delivery. Either I'm brilliant at talking to the public when drunk, or else I always sound like that.

The only other time I was ever in the same room as Steve Davis was in 1988 at the Crucible Theatre in Sheffield. I was on attachment as BBC Radio's senior producer in the north and I'd gone to watch Davis win the World Championship Final, once again against Terry Griffiths. I'd also been invited to the sponsors' dinner after the event, where, once again, there had been free champagne.

On this occasion it wasn't my job to interview Davis, but I did drink what was on offer, and at some ridiculous hour in the morning I found myself outside the Rutland Hotel in Sheffield where I was staying the night. The front door was locked so I rang the bell for the night porter. There was no answer. I walked down the road and found a phone box and rang the Rutland Hotel, but once again no response.

I then walked round the hotel until I found an open window. It led into the kitchens and I stumbled over stainless steel sinks and eventually made my way up to reception. As I entered I was confronted by the night porter, who'd obviously been woken by the noise of me coming in by unorthodox means.

He challenged me and I explained that I'd tried to ring the bell and call on the phone before showing him my room card and heading up the stairs. The following morning I asked to speak to the manager and explained what had happened. He was delighted to hear my story, telling me that he'd been trying to find an excuse to dismiss a troublesome member of staff and now I'd given him just the evidence he needed. I don't know what Steve Davis would have made of it all, but then if a more eagle-eared editor had been listening the morning after the Tolly Cobbold final, my career may have ended before I even reached Sheffield, which wouldn't have been at all "interesting," for me.

4

Brian Clough and the Handsome Young Man

My friend and colleague Pete Smith, who works for Sky TV amongst others, always greets me with a firm handshake and the words; "Morning H.Y.M." No one else knows what it means, but between us it marks the memory of a meeting in January 1993 deep in the bowels of Old Trafford, before a game between Manchester United and Nottingham Forest. It was another signpost on the road to ruin of one of our greatest football managers, Brian Clough, and it marked the last time I ever spoke to him.

The first time was 15 years earlier when Charles Harrison, my sports editor on Metro Radio in Newcastle, arranged for Clough to appear on a phone-in programme on our station. Clough had agreed for one reason and one reason only, he was being paid an awful lot of money. I'm not going to say how much, but it was around 10 per cent of what I earned in a year, and he was given dinner in a local restaurant as well. Needless to say the station more than recouped that by selling advertising, and I wasn't complaining because I was also going to have dinner with the man who'd already won the League Title with Forest and who was about to win two European Cups.

The arrangements had been made and I was looking forward to my role in the proceedings. This would be to vet the calls and then put them through so that Charles, who was presenting, could discuss them with Clough.

Then Charles decided to go away on holiday, possibly

because his current girlfriend had demanded it. His love life was always chaotic. One morning the hairdresser he was living with decided enough was enough and arrived in the car park with his belongings gathered in two suitcases. He'd not only been dumped, he'd been made homeless. However, you couldn't keep Charles down and he was such a charmer he was never without female company for long.

The upshot of this was that instead of answering the phones I'd be hosting the programme. It would be me and Brian Clough for one hour taking all the North-East public had to throw at us.

Charles had been negotiating the Clough appearance with the agent of the great man. Now it was up to me to tell him that I'd be presenting the show instead and to give him the details of transmission time and when we'd like his client to be at the studios. I also wanted to speak to Clough to establish what we'd be talking about.

"I'll run it past him and make sure that's going to be OK," the agent promised, and I told the programme controller that all seemed to be going well. He wanted confirmation though, because if we couldn't guarantee that Clough was going to be there, then we'd lose all the advertising revenue, not to mention the sports departments reputation for providing top quality programmes. I still hadn't spoken to Clough either.

On the day of the scheduled broadcast I was yet to hear back from Clough's agent. I rang him and he assured me he'd left a message for his client and that all would be fine. I relayed this to the controller, who wasn't convinced. "Tell him," he demanded, "that if we haven't heard directly from Clough by one o'clock then the programme won't be going ahead." He couldn't take the risk of a no-show.

So I told the agent, who promised he'd ask Clough to speak to us. The deadline passed and the show was called off. I rang the agent to give him the news and explained the reasons.

Ten minutes later the phone on my desk rang and I heard a familiar voice on the other end of the line.

"Hello, Brian Clough here. I understand you've called

tonight's programme off." I explained as best I could why this had happened, saying that all we needed was confirmation that he'd be appearing.

"Young man," he bellowed, "when I say I'm coming, then I'm coming. I'll see you tonight."

So the show which was on and then off was back on again and the hour flew by, with Clough in fine form. He answered the calls, made disparaging remarks about a couple of senior players during a commercial break, and when I asked him if something had merely exacerbated the situation, he gave me a withering look and said "young man, don't use long words with me." The dinner afterwards was very good as well.

Clough continued to improve Forest beyond their wildest dreams, and I moved onto other radio stations. At the BBC my esteemed colleague in the Midlands, Pat Murphy, was the man who always dealt with Mr Clough, so I rarely came across him. That was until his final season, the season when the drink finally began to tell and his genius was no longer enough to see him through.

I have two memories of that time. The first happened at Maine Road, where I was in the dressing room area prior to a game between Manchester City and Nottingham Forest. Forest's team coach pulled up outside and Clough and the players came in. Brian was very red in the face and went straight into the away dressing room, which was opposite where I was standing. A couple of minutes later he emerged, head soaking wet. It transpired that he'd had to put his head under a tap to sober up.

The second takes us to Old Trafford via a bungalow in North Yorkshire. The bungalow was owned by Ray Grant, who was Brian Clough's old teacher back in his days as a boy growing up in Middlesbrough. Indeed he was the man who'd discovered Clough as a schoolboy player and recommended him to his home town club. I'd gone to see him because Boro' had drawn Forest in the FA Cup. Ray was a sprightly, intelligent man, then well into his 80s but happy to talk about Clough the boy and Clough the manager.

At the end of the interview Ray said to me, "If you do happen to come across Brian, please send him my best wishes."

A week later, Pete Smith and I did come across Clough, wandering aimlessly along the corridor which separated the dressing rooms from the tunnel at Old Trafford. He'd obviously been drinking and was the worse for wear. Here was my chance to pass on the message.

"Brian," I said, "I was talking to Ray Grant last week and he asked me to pass on his best wishes if I should run into you." Clough stopped, turned, and said, in very slurred tones, "Thank you handsome young man. Will you pass my best wishes onto him as well?" He then staggered into the away dressing room where, I presume, he gave his pre-match team talk. Not surprisingly United won easily.

So I became the Handsome Young Man, H.Y.M. for short. I did see Clough once more a few years later. Looking grey and gaunt, he was a special guest at a televised FA Cup tie at Burton Albion, where his son Nigel was manager. He would never have remembered the H.Y.M. nor indeed the phone-in on a North-East radio station which nearly didn't happen, but like those poor contestants on *Pop Master* on Radio 2 who have to admit that they once met a minor personality, I can say that I once hosted a programme with Brian Clough and many years later acquired a nickname because of him. The nickname survives to this day, even though only two people know what it means.

5

Geoffrey Boycott and the Blonde Bombshell

On May 3rd 1979, Margaret Thatcher won a general election which was to change the direction of life in much of the United Kingdom forever. By then I'd been at Metro for nearly three years and, as well as my sports reporting, I'd started to develop other interests and turn them into radio programmes. I'd persuaded Mic Johnson to run a travel show called *On Vacation*, which ran for eight weeks just after Christmas, and which allowed many of my colleagues to go abroad on "facility trips" to make features which we would then broadcast. A local travel agent came in to add expert advice and the sales department sold plenty of advertising around it, so everyone was happy.

We'd broadcast a series around the Royal Shakespeare Company's residency at the Theatre Royal. Actors like David Suchet and Patrick Stewart had been happy to take part, and I was even able to sit in on a workshop which the cast held at my old school in Gosforth.

I'd volunteered to take part in Metro's general election programme. I'd always had an interest in psephology – the study of elections – and I'd persuaded a lecturer from Newcastle University's Department of Politics to work alongside me through the night, as we gave context to the local results, which were being handled by news editor Kevin Rowntree.

So what did all this have to do with the vociferous ex-cricketer from Yorkshire? Well on the previous evening, Geoff Boycott had been booked to appear on one of Charles

Harrison's phone-ins. My job was to drive down to Acklam Park cricket ground in Middlesbrough, where Yorkshire were playing, collect Boycott and drive him to the Metro Radio studios in Swalwell. Then I had to go to St. James' Park to cover a midweek, end-of-season game against Bristol Rovers (Newcastle won 3-0 in front of a crowd of less than 10,000).

I was a little nervous about collecting Boycott. My car had a dodgy starter motor, so there was every chance that he'd have to help me push start the thing if it refused to go. Fortunately this worry proved unfounded, even when we had to stop for fuel halfway up the A19.

Boycott was coming off his long run that evening, as he's continued to do ever since, even now as a pundit on radio and television. His subject that night was the election. Now those of you who've followed Geoffrey's career will know that he has somewhat right-wing political views. As we drove north, through the Durham coalfield which would soon become one of Thatcher's battlegrounds, he lavished praise on the soon to be Prime Minister, reserving his vitriol for Arthur Scargill, the leader of the Yorkshire Miners Union.

Much as I was taken by his political views (I just nodded and kept on driving) I was also taken by his travelling companion. She was blonde, well proportioned, I think a hairdresser from Hartlepool, and judging by the way he kept looking at her, I reckoned that later that evening their relationship was going to develop in, shall we say, a more physical way. This was probably my imagination running away with me, but it's relevant in what was about to happen.

I duly dropped the pair off in Swalwell and drove back across town to the football ground, to cover one of the least anticipated games of the season. In the press box I unpacked my equipment and set it up ready for broadcast. My colleagues in the box were only too keen to find out how my journey with Boycott had gone. So I told them about his views on Thatcher and Scargill, and most of all about the woman who was sitting alongside him in the back seat.

"Well," I said, "you should have seen the state of her,"

and then proceeded to describe her physical appearance, and the look of eager anticipation on the great cricketer's face as he thought about what might happen after the phone-in had finished.

With kick-off fast approaching I put on my headphones, ready to broadcast my preview of the game, and I could hear Charles and Geoffrey continuing to speak to those who'd called in. I identified myself and then heard a whispered voice in my ear.

"Hello Peter," it said. "It's Colin in the studio. That woman you've been talking about, well she's been sitting alongside me in the control room and she's heard every word you've said about her!"

Now fortunately for me there were no repercussions after this event. Greater broadcasters than me have lost their jobs because of things they wished they'd not said whilst they didn't realise the microphones were on. It was a cautionary tale though, and taught me a very early lesson about microphone etiquette.

I've no idea what happened to the happy couple next. I know that Newcastle United beat Bristol Rovers 3-0, and that the following night I helped preside over one of the most seismic events in British political history. I drove home in daylight, at around five o'clock in the morning, back to the cottage that Alison and I had bought earlier that month, content that my embryonic career was going somewhere. However, had Colin in the studio not given me that warning, then the next 35 years may never have happened.

My dealings with cricket since then have been sporadic, although I retain a real interest in the sport, and a devotion to *Test Match Special*. As I've detailed earlier in the book, my hero was John Arlott, and on one of the rare occasions when I actually covered a first class game, between Durham and Nottinghamshire at Trent Bridge in the one day competition, I was honoured to actually sit in the same chair the great man had recently occupied during a Test Match.

The last time I ventured into the TMS box, at Headingley,

who should be summarising but Boycott. We never spoke and I certainly wasn't going to mention that night in May 1979. I did wonder how he spent the rest of the evening mind!

6

Bobby Robson ... Without Whom

My career would not have been the same without Bobby Robson. I'd never have spent five and a half happy years living and working in Ipswich, or been given the job of BBC football producer. I may never have gone to the World Cup in Mexico or produced an eight-year long, 60 programme series about football's greatest matches if he hadn't taken part in the first one. Although he never knew it, he was by far and away the most influential sporting personality I ever met.

So much has been written about Bob, both during his life and since his death. No-one has had a bad word to say about him and I'm certainly not going to alter that. He was a part of my journalistic career, even before I ever met him. Indeed I thought I was going to meet him one Thursday evening in the late 1970s, when my sports editor on Metro Radio, Charles Harrison, received a tip off that Robson was in line to be the next manager of Sunderland, or was it Newcastle? The rumour had gathered credence when Charles discovered that a Mr B Robson was booked on a flight from Norwich to Newcastle, landing that very evening. I was dispatched to the airport to doorstep the man who was about to change the fortunes of his boyhood club, or indeed those of their deadliest rivals.

At the airport I was immediately suspicious because there were no other reporters around. This meant one of two things, it always did. Either you had a world exclusive, or, more likely, you'd turned up at the wrong time, in the wrong place and there was no story. There was someone waiting for him, he had a sign with his name on it, but he was a taxi driver and Mr Robson turned out to be a pig farmer from Haltwhistle, amused by the confusion, but certainly not the man we'd hoped for.

Shortly afterwards, Mr Robson was also not the man Sunderland turned to when a Press conference was called at Roker Park to announce the successor to Ken Knighton. The assembled hacks were looking forward to speaking to Robson, a Geordie who'd transformed Ipswich Town, when in walked Billy Elliott, one time Sunderland player but more recently managing some club in Norway.

"Hello Billy," said one of my more senior colleagues, "have you come to meet Bobby as well?"

The answer came as something of a shock, "No, I'm the new Sunderland manager." He didn't last very long and later went on to fail at Darlington as well. Bobby Robson remained resolutely at Portman Road, refusing once more the opportunity to return to his native North-East. That would be for another time.

So in the autumn of 1980 I took a dramatic career step. If Bobby Robson wasn't going to come from Suffolk to the North-East, then I'd go to Ipswich to join him instead. A job had come up on Radio Orwell, a small commercial station in the town. They wanted a sports editor whose job, amongst other things, would involve covering Ipswich Town wherever they played. At that time they were top of Division One, and in the UEFA Cup. There were other reasons for wanting to move of course. It was the right stage of my career and my wife wanted to move closer to her parents, but the main reason was that Bobby Robson's football team was the best in the land.

They had two mercurial Dutchmen: Arnold Muhren and Frans Thijssen pulling the midfield strings, defenders like Mick Mills and Terry Butcher, and two strikers in Paul Mariner and Alan Brazil who scored goals for fun.

Having successfully applied for the job, I moved to Suffolk in January 1981 and went to watch my first game at Portman Road. Ipswich beat Birmingham City 5-1 and afterwards I rather nervously waited for Robson to hold court at his post-match press conference before introducing myself to him. In a vain attempt to ingratiate myself I mentioned one or two journalist acquaintances who'd asked to be remembered to him. He hadn't a clue who I was on about. I then told him that I'd been recommended to come to Suffolk by a former Ipswich manager, Jackie Milburn, who I'd been privileged to know in my four years on Metro. Bob's face immediately softened. I think I'd passed my first test.

So for the next 18 months I must have interviewed Bobby Robson pretty much every week. On a Friday morning I'd walk down from the studios at Electric House, down Lloyds Avenue and Princess Street, then along the back of the Churchmans Stand to the reception of Ipswich Town Football Club. Pat Godbold, Bobby's secretary, would find out where he was and I'd be ushered in to speak to him. If you wanted three minutes he'd talk for ten, if you wanted a 30-second sound bite, his first answer would go on for three minutes. That was Bob all over, often reticent to speak, "Can't you find one of the players today Pete?" then off on one of his rambling answers. The players used to nickname him "Maurice" short for Maurice Mogadon, because his team talks would go on so long they'd send them to sleep. But they would have done anything for him.

It was a glorious time to be in Ipswich. The Speedway team won the double and Ipswich Town came back from Amsterdam with the UEFA Cup. All that summer though, the question was "would Bobby Robson stay, or would he move on?" I wanted him to stay, since he was the reason I'd gone there in the first place. At the time Manchester United were looking for a new manager and it seemed that he was one of the front runners. In the end he stayed for one more season before leaving what he described to me as "the best job in England," for "the most important job in England." Bobby Robson had taken over from Ron Greenwood as manager of the national team.

It meant a sometimes daily commute from his house on Constitution Hill, 75 minutes each way on the train to Liverpool Street. Still, he found time to give me an interview to preview the start of the new league season in August 1982, something he continued to do for me until I left Radio Orwell three years later and started to do the same commute as him. In our separate ways we had to leave one sort of paradise in order to further our careers.

In the summer of 1985 I'd joined the BBC and was sent on my Production "A" course. As part of it I had to produce a half hour documentary and I remembered something Bobby had said, about swapping the best job for the most important job. I telephoned Pat at Portman Road and asked if she'd put it to Bobby that I'd like to make the programme about him and the differences between managing Ipswich and England. I added that it would be for internal use only. Pat called back to tell me that Mr. Robson would be happy for me to go ahead, so on the middle Saturday of Wimbledon fortnight I sat in his front room as Elsie served tea and biscuits and he gave me the sort of interview other journalists could only dream of.

I also spoke with Terry Butcher, later to become captain of England, and Donald Saunders of the *Daily Telegraph*, one of the most respected sportswriters of the day. Pleased with the final programme I sent a copy to my head of sport, Pat Ewing, and returned to the course. A couple of days later I was summoned to her office. The current football producer had just announced he was leaving and Pat wanted me to take over. I still believe that if Bobby Robson hadn't agreed to do the documentary, then I may not have been offered a job which has occupied me one way or another for the rest of my career.

Within a year Bobby Robson was posing for a photograph in my hotel room with the minister for sport and the British ambassador to Mexico. The room was in Saltillo, where the England team was based during the qualifying stages of the 1986 World Cup. Back then the players and the press shared the same accommodation, and whilst we didn't eat together it was quite possible to stop Glenn Hoddle or Peter Reid as they walked across the garden and ask for a quick interview. Sometimes players would drop by to take part in programmes. Mark Hateley joined us for the opening ceremony, I interviewed Gary Lineker on the end of my bed, and Gary Bailey spent most of the two weeks sitting in my armchair talking on the telephone to his surgeon as he pondered the knee injury which would herald the end of his career.

For Bobby it was a traumatic time. The team lost their opening game, drew against Morocco and were on the verge of coming home until Lineker scored a hat-trick against Poland to catapult him to stardom and take England into the knockout stages. Had they not won that afternoon then Bobby Robson's career would probably have ended there and then. He'd been feeling the strain, as photographs of the time showed. He was an emotional man often at his best in moments of adversity, sometimes arrogant when successful. The weight of the world seemed on his shoulders at times in Saltillo, and it was only Lineker, and later Maradona, who enhanced his reputation.

Interviewing him in the concrete bunker next to the Monterey dressing rooms after the first two games was tough. He couldn't explain how things had gone wrong, although his blind loyalty to an injury prone Bryan Robson hadn't helped him. But a week later I have another photo of Bobby, trouser leg rolled up, laughing as he waits to be interviewed live on BBC Radio in what appears to be my hotel bathroom in Mexico City. We'd come a long way since that embarrassing introduction in Ipswich just five years before.

Between Mexico and Robson's great triumph in Italy in 1990 came the disastrous European Football Championship Finals in Germany in 1988. England played three and lost the lot. Bobby Robson went home before I did, that's how bad it was, although Arnold Muhren, one of his Ipswich protégées, did play on the winning Dutch team in the final. Later that year England played a friendly in Riyadh against Saudi Arabia. They drew 1-1 and the tabloid headlines the following morning said, in both English and Arabic: "In the name of Allah, go." That was how low Bobby Robson's stock was then, and even as I interviewed him on the pitch at the end of the game I wondered if his days as manager were numbered. How wrong I was.

England qualified for Italia 90, and based themselves in Sardinia. By then I'd moved back north and so viewed the next

World Cup from a producers chair in Rome. Our paths wouldn't cross again for some while, although in 1992 Bobby did spend time giving me an interview from his house in Portugal, talking about Ipswich Town's UEFA Cup triumph of 1981. It was for the opening programme in a series about great British club triumphs. Bob Shennan, now controller of BBC Radio 2, commissioned four shows. We called them *Glory Nights*, and I went on to make dozens, about European triumphs, FA Cup winners and giant-killers, which the embryonic Radio 5 Live broadcast on Monday nights throughout the 1990s. But once again, having Bobby Robson on the very first show helped set the bar high, and because he appeared others followed.

By now, Bobby was coaching abroad, and enjoying success, but in 1999 after spending time in Holland, Portugal and Spain, Bobby Robson came home. He came home to the job he'd probably wanted more than any other, more than England, more than Barcelona. Bobby Robson became manager of Newcastle United.

At the time I was covering Formula One as well as football. Indeed I'd been in the paddock at Spa in Belgium when my mobile rang and the office told me that Ruud Gullit had been sacked at St. James' Park. The following week Bobby was appointed as his successor, and I made sure I was there to report the event. As the BBC Radio representative I was ushered into a private box to await my turn to interview the new manager. The Newcastle hierarchy didn't know that I knew Bob, and I wasn't going to let on. So when my turn came and he walked into what he thought was going to be just another anonymous interview his smile lit up the room. He greeted me like a long lost friend, and all he could say to the assembled PR's and press officers was "He was with me in Ipswich, he was with me in Ipswich." Couldn't remember my name mind, but the recognition meant so much. My first question to him was obvious. "Bob, you once told me that managing Ipswich Town was the best job in England and that managing the England team was the most important. Where does the Newcastle job rate?" Good question, I just wish I could remember his answer.

Over the next five years, when my motor racing commitments allowed, I'd head off up to Newcastle to speak to the great man. He never disappointed despite often showing his usual "Oh do I have to," expression before giving the typical Robson interview we all loved.

In August 2004 Freddie Shepherd sacked Bobby, believing that the dressing room no longer respected him. I'm sure it broke his heart, especially given the chaos which followed. Like only Joe Harvey and Kevin Keegan before him, Bobby Robson knew what football meant to the people of Tyneside and they loved him for it. He never stopped loving them back, as his work for his cancer charity showed. Bob had been diagnosed with nasal cancer and had had to have a false palate inserted which he had to take out, clean and re-insert, not an easy task. I always felt that he was quite a vain man, and it must have been very difficult for him to tolerate such an inconvenience.

Far from letting the cancer diminish him, it gave him a sense of purpose, and the Bobby Robson Cancer Trust raised, and still raises, millions of pounds for the unit at Newcastle's Freeman Hospital which bears his name. Time after time Bobby Robson recovered from cancer, but in the end there was no way back. Sir Bobby Robson, now a Knight of the Realm thanks to Tony Blair, was dying.

In July 2009 I saw Bob for the last time. In a game for his charity at St. James' Park, England played Germany, and before kick-off the great man was wheeled along the touchline to shake hands with all those players who'd come to Newcastle to support him. Gazza and Shearer, Stuart Pearce and Peter Shilton, no-one had refused the invitation. In the stands were those who'd come a long way with Bobby Robson, people like Charlie Woods, one of his loyal lieutenants, who'd worked with him in Ipswich and in Newcastle. Charlie admitted to me before the game that Bobby's health wasn't the best. You could see that on the pitch, he was frail but he was still smiling, loving being with football people.

On that Sunday summer afternoon on the pitch where he used to watch Newcastle United as a small boy on an afternoon trip from Langley Park, Sir Bobby Robson acknowledged the crowd, waving to all four corners of the ground. He was waving goodbye and I was honoured to have been there. Five days later he lost his battle with cancer and English football lost one of its all-time greats. I'd been lucky enough to know Bob for 28 years, during which time he'd experienced as much disappointment as triumph and borne both equally. He'd also had an incalculable effect on my career. He may not have always remembered my name, but without him I may not have had a name worth remembering.

7

Fergie, His Rants in My Earhole

It may surprise you to know that of all the many football managers I've interviewed, few have been more co-operative than Sir Alex Ferguson.

Yes, he's had a go at me (of which more later) but over the 15 years in which it was my job to speak to him, I always found Fergie happy to talk, and good value, even in defeat.

My first contact came in the autumn of 1981. I was sports editor of Radio Orwell in Ipswich, and Ipswich Town, the UEFA Cup holders, had been drawn to start their defence against Aberdeen, managed at that time by Alex. As soon as the draw had been made I called Pittodrie and asked to speak to the manager. He answered his office phone and said "I suppose you want to talk about the cup draw?" and then gave me an excellent few minutes for the sports desk.

The first leg was at Portman Road and Ipswich had leant Aberdeen their team bus to take them to their training session on the morning of the game. I planned to interview Ferguson after the session and arrived just in time to see the bus pulling out of the ground en route to the Belstead Brook Hotel where they were staying. I'd missed him.

I followed that bus like a policeman tailing a get-away car and arrived at the hotel just in time to miss the staff and players making for their rooms. What was I to do? I had to have that interview but the manager had already gone upstairs. So I asked reception to call him so I could put my request to him directly. He answered the phone in his room, and after I made my apologies for disturbing him I asked if he would grant me the two or three minutes I needed to save my skin. Fergie couldn't have been more polite and after a short wait he came downstairs and gave me a perfect interview.

Later that day, after Aberdeen managed a creditable 1-1 draw, I remember how assured the young manager was as he came into the foyer at the ground and conducted his press conference. Mel Henderson, who was the Ipswich PRO, just looked at me and said, "Now that's the way to do it." We were both impressed by Ferguson's self-confidence.

A couple of weeks later, Alex and his assistant Archie Knox played host to the visiting Ipswich press, delighted to see us on their patch, and even supplying excellent gin and tonics from the boardroom bar. The hospitality didn't carry over to the game the following night, when Aberdeen knocked the holders out of the competition.

Fast forward five years, to November 1986. I was by then BBC Radio's football producer and on November 22nd I was in charge of our outside broadcast at Old Trafford, where Manchester United were playing Queens Park Rangers. It was the first home game in charge for United's new manager, the very same Alex Ferguson who I'd encountered in Ipswich and Aberdeen.

United won 1-0, with a goal from the Danish International John Siveback, and after the game I went looking for the perfect *Sports Report* sequence. This meant that Peter Jones would provide the match report, and at the end of it be able to say: "And Alex Ferguson, the new Manchester United manager, is speaking to Mike Ingham." By then I'd have hoped to have Ferguson with us at our interview position, after which Mike would conduct the interview. What actually happened was that Fergie came out of the dressing room too early, just as the theme music to *Sports Report* was fading away, and James Alexander Gordon (JAG) was about to start reading the football results. I had two options. One was to keep the manager waiting until the results were finished so that we could talk to him live, the other was to record the interview at our control point, then hope the engineers could rewind the tape and have it ready to play. All this had to be done before Peter Jones started his match report. We were up against the clock, with maybe four minutes to play with. This was the option I chose, and to this day I often wonder if I'd gone the other way, whether Ferguson would have stayed to do the interview.

So the engineers rolled the tape, Mike Ingham started his interview and I could hear Mike and Fergie in one ear, JAG in the other. Would we be able to finish the interview, tell Peter Jones to cue it in, and turn it round in time? This was in the days before digital when everything works within a split second, but Fergie was in good form and I didn't fancy telling Mike to wind things up. As we descended into Divisions Three and Four, with Newport County playing Middlesbrough and Darlington at home to Wigan, I was beginning to worry. Into Division Four and the interview is still going. Mike knows that we're up against time and in fact he thinks I've made a bad call here and is probably in no mood to save my skin. In Division Four the last scoreline was Wolverhampton Wanderers 0 Wrexham 3, and so we were into the Scottish results. I wanted to tell Alex that his old Aberdeen had beaten Rangers 1-0, but I was more concerned about winding the interview up. Before we reached Fine Fare Division Two, with Alloa, Cowdenbeath, Stenhousemuir and the rest, the interview mercifully drew to a close. With seconds to spare I thanked the new manager, gave him the news from Pittodrie, told Peter Jones what to do, and made sure the engineers kept their part of the bargain.

It all worked smoothly. *Sports Report* sounded like it always did, and still does. It was slick and professional, giving the listeners the big news of the day with the important interviews. Of course back in 1986 none of us had any idea that Ferguson would go on to achieve all he has at Old Trafford. It's perhaps interesting to see how he's adapted to the changes in the media. Nowadays BBC Radio has to fight even harder for the top live interviews, we're still "in the tunnel," but then so are any number of TV cameras and club websites, not to mention a whole army of press officers, who can range from the helpful to the simply obstructive. For eight years, of course, Ferguson chose not to speak to the Corporation at all, years when I was mainly away doing other things and didn't come across him. But from that first Old Trafford moment in 1986 until I went off to do Formula One a decade later, I probably interviewed him more than any other manager, and probably more often than any other broadcaster.

Before Manchester United moved out to Carrington in the late 1990s, a fortress through whose gates only the privileged or accredited are allowed, we used to gather down at the The Cliff, United's training ground in Lower Broughton. Once you'd knocked on the gates and Harold the security man had let you in, you could stop players in the car park and talk to them, whilst Alex would conduct his pre-match press conference in the downstairs reception, often still wearing his woolly hat and tracksuit. It was there, one day in the early 1990s, that he contributed to my series called *Glory Nights*, about Aberdeen's European Cup-Winners Cup triumph of 1983. He sat there for 20 minutes and reminisced about the famous match against Bayern Munich when Gordon Strachan deceived the Germans with a clever free-kick, John Hewitt's star jumps and the civic reception on Union Street. He was in his element, as he always is when talking about football.

The night United celebrated winning the title, I remember being in the bowels of Old Trafford, doing live interviews for our programme, and seeing Alex across a crowded tunnel. I waved at him, trusted my luck and told the studio to come over even though I had no-one to talk to. As they cued me Ferguson came alongside and I was able to ask him something along the lines of "What does it feel like to be a king?"

Once the team were in Europe I travelled to many exotic and not so exotic places with them. He trusted me to the extent of even asking me who certain people were on the flights back after the game, and he never ducked an interview, even when his heart couldn't have been in it. After Torpedo Moscow beat United in a penalty shoot-out in the pouring Russian rain he came straight out to perform his post-match duties. They'd been knocked out in the First Round of the UEFA Cup. He wouldn't let that happen again.

At Old Trafford we even used to develop a strategy of talking on his way from the written press conference back to the dressing rooms. The walk was usually just long enough to give me what I needed.

At Wembley I had to stand and wait down the long tunnel, listening to the cheering fans after a Cup Final win, and then look up to the pitch to spot Fergie coming down towards the dressing rooms. My job was to stop him and conduct a live interview. If ever my innards turned to water, this was the time and the place. It was like asking the best looking girl in the room for a dance and just hoping she'd say yes. Alex would invariably stop, because he knew I'd be able to tell him how his beloved Glasgow Rangers had done. After that it was easy.

However, few escape the hair dryer, and it happened to me at Bramall Lane in Sheffield, after Eric Cantona had dumped Sheffield United out of the FA Cup.

Along with the other radio reporters I gathered round for a routine post-match interview, not knowing that Ferguson was unhappy with something that BBC Radio 5 Live had broadcast. He saw me and came at me with both barrels. There were more four letter words in a 30 second outburst than I think I've ever heard before or since. He told me what he thought of my radio station, of the reporter who'd put together a piece about Ryan Giggs, and said that he wouldn't be speaking to us again anytime soon.

At the end of the tirade, he calmed down and uttered the words I'll never forget; "It's nothing personal Peter, but you can still f*** off." That ban was eventually resolved by me talking to Alex on a flight between Manchester and Glasgow, where we just happened to be sitting a row apart. If you had the courage to meet him face-to-face you always stood a better chance.

In 1997 I stopped producing and went off to cover Formula One. I watched Manchester United win the European Cup in a bar on the Costa Brava, and rarely came into contact with Fergie. On the rare occasions when we did meet, like at a Budapest baggage carousel, he'd always talk to me, usually to moan about Alan Green. This was when the ban was firmly in place, and it really soured my opinion of United in general and Ferguson in particular. I'd only ever be allowed to see him at UEFA press conferences, when he'd always acknowledge my presence, presumably the ban was still "nothing personal."

Before he retired Ferguson was back on the *Match of the Day* screens and on the 5 Live airwaves, which is as it should be. I can't see things returning to the time when I could call the manager at Old Trafford to see if he'd be available to work as a summariser for BBC Radio. If I followed the United team bus back to their hotel I'd probably be stopped by muscular security men with a different agenda before I could call the manager's room to ask for an interview. Manchester United has become just too big to allow that. Players walk past journalists now with their iPods on and their own personal security. It only ever happens in English football. The rest of Europe and The World, and other sports in this country, accept that the media has a job to do and behave in a professional way towards us. Manchester United players treat my colleagues and myself with contempt, which is why most of the media dislike them. It's a far cry from gin and tonics in the Pittodrie Boardroom, but however we've reached this stage, at least I know it was nothing personal.

8

Driving the Back Roads of France
with Mika Hakkinen

In the summer of 1992 a splendid BBC features producer
called Alistair Wilson gave me some money to go and make a
documentary. He took the cash from a "pilot budget" which
allowed broadcasters the chance to produce the programme
and then see if it could find a place on the air.

A couple of years before I'd put together a fly-on-the-wall
piece about Oldham Athletic. I'd followed them from their
photo call on the first day back for pre-season training until
their first game, which they lost. Radio Four had broadcast
it in their *Sound Track* series, and it had been well received.
This was to be a similar exercise except that football was being
replaced by Formula One motor racing. I'd arranged to travel
to the French Grand Prix at Magny Cours with the Lotus team.
They weren't the wealthiest in the paddock, which was why
I found myself on a Wednesday morning in deepest Norfolk,
boarding a bus to take myself, the mechanics, and one of the
drivers, all the way to the middle of France.

The driver on the bus was Johnny Herbert, later to win
three Grands Prix for Benetton and Stewart. We immediately
settled down to the journey, playing endless games of Trivial
Pursuit, with Johnny showing a complete lack of knowledge
about several things, notably parts of the human body. As we
travelled I got to know the people who'd be key to me making
my programme over the next five days. There was John Miles,
son of Lord Bernard Miles, jazz fan and owner of his own record
label. Paul Diggins, the chief mechanic, known to everyone as

"Drez," for reasons I can't go into here. There were the caterers and the engineers, the tyre men and the computer geeks, all on their way to the race.

The journey was long. Norfolk to Central France would take around 12 hours, but the interviews were stacking up and the programme was well on its way.

The hotels near Magny Cours are quite poor and we were staying in one of them. By Thursday morning the troops were already tired, and morale wasn't helped by the news that French lorry drivers had decided to blockade the circuit as a protest against high fuel prices. This meant that there was no petrol for the racing cars and that the bus couldn't travel to the track on the main N7.

There are alternative ways to reach the Magny Cours Circuit but if you're staying to the north of the town of Nevers they're not that easy to find. Even when you do find them, negotiating them in a coach full of grumpy Lotus team personnel is even harder.

At one point, with the party completely lost, John Miles and myself were trying to converse in rudimentary French with a local who I was convinced had told us to "venez a gauche," to the left. John was convinced he'd actually said "a droite," which was entirely in the opposite direction. To add to our troubles every other vehicle seemed to be using the same back lanes, and when you're trying to reverse a bus with several angry French motorists right up your bumper, you can appreciate that by the time we reached the circuit, late, frustrated, hot and bothered, the team was not in the best of moods.

Still, they had three Formula One cars to prepare, one for each of the drivers plus the spare car, which was only used if one of the first two was damaged. Johnny Herbert disappeared to the motor home to speak with his race engineer and I reviewed the material I'd already obtained. Some of it was very good, especially John Miles trying to convince everyone that we had to turn left, or was it right. Paul Bussey, the team manager, was on the telephone trying to organise the delivery of fuel for the cars, which, because of the blockade, now had to be shipped from England, at enormous cost. No-one had a minute to spare, which created a problem, since the other driver, who'd arrived that morning from Monaco, was currently in his hotel to the north of Nevers, and was needed for the afternoon team briefings with his engineer Andy Tilley.

The driver was a young Finn named Mika Hakkinen. I'd met him once at a winter test in Norfolk, and was about to meet him again under very different circumstances. Since everyone else had things to do, Paul suggested I drive one of the hire cars, a Fiat Punto to be precise, and collect Hakkinen and bring him to the circuit.

So off I went, arriving at the hotel via the back lanes and trying hard to remember the route for our return journey. Mika didn't seem to be bothered that a radio reporter had been sent to pick him up. In the decade which followed, Mika never seemed to be too bothered about anything other than driving a car very fast, which was something he now intended to do as he took the Punto's keys from me. I had to sit in the passenger seat.

Now I don't know how many of you have ever travelled through the back lanes of Central France with a Formula One driver at the wheel of a small Italian hire car, but it's certainly an experience like no other. You just sit tight and hope, whilst barking out instructions about which way to go.

"Mika, we're just coming to the village of … oh, we've just gone through the village of," and "turn right in 200 metres … oh, you just did."

Hakkinen seemed oblivious to oncoming traffic, passing between them and the hedge with centimetres to spare. He anticipated the twists and the turns before I had chance to even tell him about them, and whilst I don't think I've ever travelled so fast, I felt strangely safe, because here was one of the best drivers in the world. He was also, as they all do, showing off.

Mika went on to win two World Titles with McClaren of course, titles I was privileged to witness. By then he was one of the most famous sportsmen in the world, but I don't think he ever forgot the reporter who came to collect him and I always felt completely at ease when interviewing him, which I did many times later in both our careers.

Meanwhile back at the Magny Cours circuit it was still 1992, the lorry drivers were still blockading the N7, and Mika and Andy had more pressing things on their mind, like walking the track together on a lovely summer evening and allowing me to walk with them. They examined every corner and camber, where the gear changes were needed, could there be a chance of overtaking. Andy once told me that he was Mika's conscience, making sure that the Finn didn't take a risk too many. Mika was just the taciturn Scandinavian, with a really dry sense of humour.

That weekend in France, Lotus provided me with a story I couldn't have scripted. Yes, Nigel Mansell won the race, but Hakkinen finished fourth and Herbert sixth, points for both drivers and the team's best result for years.

By Sunday night I had more than enough material, and didn't really fancy the long bus trip back. At this point Linden Swainston, who organised F1 travel, offered me a place on the charter flight going from Clermont-Ferrand to Stanstead. I then managed to cadge a lift back to Norfolk with the Lotus team Principals Peter Collins and Peter Wright. The only leg of the journey I hadn't sorted was how to drive the 70 miles from the circuit to Clermont-Ferrand Airport. Paul Bussey had a solution.

He said there was a spare seat in the back of a Fiat Punto hire car, possible the same one I'd travelled the lanes in with Mika Hakkinen. The good news on this occasion was that Mika wasn't driving. The bad news was that he was navigating and Johnny Herbert was behind the wheel. As we drove to the airport, the team-mates had just two aims. One was to find a McDonalds, the second was to throw water bombs at whoever they recognised. Johnny Herbert was particularly keen on this. The fact that he was driving didn't seem to bother him, and he had plenty of supplies, since the boys had managed to take on board several bottles of Evian.

Johnny was pretty much the most reckless driver I've ever

travelled with. I cowered in the back as he sprayed anyone who came within reach whilst Hakkinen became obsessed with spotting the famous golden arches so he could find the burger he so desperately craved.

Eventually we ran out of water and found the restaurant. McDonalds was giving away a bum bag with each meal bought, and since Mika didn't have any children and I had two, he gave me his. Somewhere in our house I'm sure there's still this free gift, donated by someone my small children (they were five and two at the time) had never heard of. Many years later, when Mika won the World Title and my son became an F1 fanatic, it would have been something to treasure, but by then it was lost.

Since 1992 I've had dinner with Johnny Herbert in a revolving restaurant in Montreal and interviewed Mika at the end of his last ever race in the darkness of the paddock in Suzuka. I once bizarrely followed Johnny Herbert through security at Frankfurt Airport, hours after he'd won the European Grand Prix at the Nurburgring. He kept setting off the alarms, even after he'd taken off his shoes and his belt, his coat and his jumper. Johnny wasn't flustered, this sort of thing happened to him all the time.

"I keep telling them I've got so much metal pinning my legs together," he said, "but they don't seem to understand. Bet Schumacher wouldn't have this much trouble!"

Ah, Michael Schumacher, that's another chapter entirely. For now I salute Hakkinen and Herbert, and that pilot documentary, which I'm delighted to say was eventually aired on BBC Radio 5 Live. But I wouldn't recommend letting them drive you anywhere, especially through the back lanes of France.

9

Ross Brawn and the Football Dinner

During my first season covering Formula One in 1997, Nick Harris organised a football dinner. Nick is an ever cheerful writer and broadcaster, Oxford United fan and all round good bloke, and like many of us on the motor racing beat, come the middle of August he'd rather have been reporting on football on a Saturday afternoon than watching a Formula 3000 race and going to Ron Dennis's usual press get together in the McClaren hospitality facility.

Nick was working for one of the main sponsors of the Williams team at that time, and along with their marketing manager, Jim Wright, himself a Watford season ticket holder, decided to organise a dinner to celebrate the start of the new football season. The inaugural event was held at one of Budapest's best known restaurants, famous for its entrance, which hadn't been repaired since a Soviet tank had rammed it during the 1956 uprising.

Jonathan Legard and I joined several members of the ITV crew, including their editor, Crystal Palace supporter Neil Duncanson, for an evening which concluded with the resident gypsy band playing the theme to *Match of the Day*, whilst we stood on our chairs singing along.

Once started, the football dinner began to gather momentum. The following year it was decreed that all attendees should wear replica shirts, and whilst not everyone did, die-hards like the *Sunday Times'* Adam Parsons and ITV's Jim Rosenthal answered the call, representing West Ham and Oxford United respectively. We were almost joined by a member of the Royal Family, but Peter Phillips, who was dining in the same restaurant, chose to stay with his guests rather than coming across to express his love for Tottenham Hotspur. However he was amused by our rendition of the football theme, and I reckoned that he'd rather wished he could have been with us.

By 1999, a number of important things had happened. The restaurant we used had closed down, and Nick Harris had stopped covering Formula One. A new management team for the FOFIFO (Fans of Football in Formula One) dinner had been formed, by myself and *Motorsport News* columnist Simon Arron, self-confessed Altrincham fanatic and fluent French speaker. The rules were tightened so that replica shirt wearing was now compulsory, and we changed venues to Becketts Irish Bar. We also introduced "The Speech", where each invitee had to speak about their team's current situation and their hopes for the new season. We also brought in the Predictions Competition, where each guest had to announce their nominations for title winners, relegation from and promotion to the Premiership, and First Premiership managerial casualty. We even had a tie-break, which was the date of that first casualty.

At our first Becketts dinner we'd also acquired some silverware, provided by a bookmaking firm who'd become involved in F1, and who were quite happy to donate the E.I.Addio Trophy for the winner. They also picked up the bar bill if I remember rightly. Around the table that night were some of Fleet Street's finest, real football men like Derrick Allsop, whose love of Manchester United was well known, the *Daily Express's* Bob McKenzie, who couldn't find an Ayr United shirt so made one using black felt tip pen on a plain white tee-shirt. Kevin Eason of *The Times* represented Middlesbrough, The *Daily Mail's* Ray Matts had a special West Bromwich Albion shirt with his name on the back, and the Press Association's Ian Gordon, another Old Trafford red who, for some reason, wore a Boca Juniors shirt. We had two of F1's top photographers, Darren Heath and Mark Thompson, Darren a West Ham season ticket holder, and Thommo who followed Northampton Town through thick and thin. My colleague Jonathan Legard, probably Chester City's most famous supporter was also there, as was Simon Arron, who couldn't find an Altrincham shirt, so who wore a France top and was forced to make his speech in French.

We had team members as well, from Williams and Arrows, as well as our sponsor, an Arsenal fan, and the evening was a resounding success. I kept the prediction forms, and by the end of the season worked out that Jim Rosenthal had won. Becketts had kept the trophy, promising to have it engraved with the winners name for presentation in August. I rang the manager and explained what needed doing.

ME: "That's Jim Rosenthal, R-O-S-E-N-T-H-A-L, I spelled it out for him."

HIM: "No problem Mr Slater, we'll have Mr Rosenthal's name on it for the night of the dinner.

Sure enough, when the 20 or so guests arrived at Becketts, there was the trophy, engraved TIM Rosenthal.

By now we'd also acquired a member of F1's elite. He was a genuine football fan, born and brought up in Salford, a graduate of Manchester Grammar School and a Manchester United supporter so keen that he'd bought a subscription to MUTV for his house in Marinello, where he was Ferrari's technical director. Because by the start of the new century I'd persuaded Ross Brawn that the Saturday night before the Hungarian Grand Prix was just the time to spend with a bunch of fanatics at the FOFIFO Dinner.

I should also mention at this juncture the presence of Mr Kevin Garside. Kevin first came to the dinner when he was standing in for the regular correspondent of the *Daily Mirror*. He enjoyed the experience so much that he changed newspapers and became the motor racing correspondent of the *Daily Telegraph*.

Kevin comes from Oldham and during his first speech at the dinner, he made the fatal error of admitting that he'd walked past Boundary Park on his way to catch the bus to Old Trafford. He was a Manchester United fan who'd started following them instead of his local team. We gave him unmitigated abuse. Bread rolls were thrown, every time he stood up we told him to sit down, every time he sat down we ordered him to stand up. Kevin being Kevin he took it all, dished it back, and returned for more. It became the highlight of the evening. From then on the Garside Speech became the final act of any FOFIFO gathering, and when we moved venues a couple of years later, baskets of stale bread were supplied specially.

So I'd invited Ross Brawn and wondered if he'd turn up. He even promised to bring his wife Jean along, which was fine by us, as our female representation was limited up till then by Di from ITV, who spoke about her son's school football team. We decided to put the Brawns in the Manchester United corner, along with Allsop and Garside, Simon and I thinking that perhaps the Ferrari chief might not make it, because of a technical meeting with Michael Schumacher.

Inside the back room of Becketts that night the mood quickly became quite boisterous. Robert Watherston of Honda had turned up resplendent in the green and white hoops of Celtic, Nigel Green from Arrows had managed to buy the new Aldershot top, and I'd turned up proudly wearing an actual Newcastle United shirt, given to be by the stadium manager at St. James' Park. I still have it, it has the number 21 on the back. I think it belonged to Carl Serrant, who played just six games for my team, but what do I care! Even Simon Arron had raided the Altrincham Super Store, so he was going to speak in English this year.

Then, to cheers and applause, in walked Ross Brawn. Not only had he turned up, he'd brought Jean with him, and both were wearing the new Manchester United shirts. They'd even filled in the Predictions Quiz. Here was someone who had really entered into the spirit of the evening and the event. When time came for the speeches Ross even stood up, told a filthy joke which would have upset Liverpool supporters in particular, and told us just why United would win the league ... again!

Just like he predicted, United did win the league again.

On the track Ferrari were untouchable, and when I came to add up the points tally Ross Brawn had won the Predictions Competition. Armed with the information I went to find Ross at the next Grand Prix and gave him the good news. The tie break question had been to give the date of the first Premiership managerial sacking. Ross told me he'd worked it out by looking at the fixtures and seeing which clubs had tricky starts to the season, then deciding exactly which defeat would be the final straw for some trigger happy chairman. No wonder he was one of the highest paid and most successful men in the sport!

So Ross was presented with his trophy, surrounded by the usual suspects. Even James Allan, ITV's F1 commentator and a season ticket holder at Anfield toasted his success. After the ritual throwing of bread rolls at Kevin Garside the evening began to wind down. That was until the door to the back room opened and in walked Eddie Jordan. I can't quite remember the sequence of events, but I know it involved first of all a heated discussion between EJ and Bob McKenzie, then Eddie picking up the E.I.Addio Trophy and throwing it across the room, where it was superbly fielded by Derrick Allsop low to his right. The night was pronounced a success.

With the Brawns on board and Vodafone sponsoring both Manchester United and Ferrari, the next move was to bring the dinner into the F1 Paddock. Vodafone agreed to organise the event in their motorhome and we also brought it forward to the Thursday night, a much quieter evening in the F1 weekend. More people wanted to attend, from all areas of the paddock. We had a Jaguar mechanic whose devotion to Everton was well known, and one year Steve Rider, a Charlton Athletic supporter, was invited at the last minute and went out to buy a Ujpest Dosza shirt, so that he didn't look out of place. RTL Television from Germany was so fascinated by the concept of the dinner that they made a feature about it.

By now the speeches had taken on a life of their own. Mark Thompson would always serenade Northampton Town in verse. Derrick Allsop defended Manchester United one night by wearing not one, but five shirts, which he proceeded to take off one by one to demonstrate his life-long support for the team. He did that on one of the hottest nights of the year, and drew a standing ovation. Ian Gordon continued to wear a different shirt every year, and Jonathan Legard grew more and more morose as his beloved Chester City disappeared from the League.

Then one night, round about the time I was finishing my eight year stint in the sport, one of the Vodafone team, wearing his Manchester United shirt, made a fatal error. He stood up and told us why he was a "dedicated" follower of the team. It transpired that he was born in Switzerland, grew up in London with parents who had no allegiance to Manchester, and started supporting them because he'd "seen them on the telly."

It was like a red rag to a bull for the next speaker, the head of Cosworth Engineering, Bernard Ferguson. Bernard had had a more traditional upbringing, and wore his claret and blue shirt with pride.

"I was born in Burnley," he announced to great cheers. "My mother came from … Burnley." More cheers. "My father came from … Burnley, and I support … Burnley." The cheers echoed down the paddock, from McClaren to Minardi. Any stragglers heading back to their Budapest hotels would have been left in no doubt as to which side this strange, eclectic dinner party was on.

Sometimes Formula One can become a bit too pompous for its own good. There are too many who are too full of their own importance, usually those flitting round the periphery of the sport. At the centre of it all, in the hospitality kitchens and the back of the garages, in the press room and, fortunately, on that Ferrari pit wall, are enough who don't fall into that category. People who'll have a cup of tea with you on a hot afternoon, who'll chew the fat over a beer in some local bar, away from the madness, some who'll don a replica football shirt, write poems about their team, throw bread rolls at Kevin Garside and simply enjoy each others company. The FOFIFO Dinner represented all that for me. The mechanic and the journalist, the marketing man and the photographer, the technical director of Ferrari and his wife, all united for one night. I thank Ross and Jean Brawn for being "one of the lads", and Bernard Ferguson for a speech I'll never forget. Oh, and Kevin Garside, for just being there.

10

Gary Lineker's Sitting on the Edge of My Bed

In the early summer of 1986 I was in Mexico for the World Cup. More precisely I was in a luxury hotel on the outskirts of Saltillo, itself a 45 minute drive from Monterey, where the England football team were due to play the first three group matches of their campaign.

I'd arrived with the BBC's football correspondent Bryon Butler, and we had adjoining rooms, linked by a through door. My room had a broadcast box which we used to send material to the International Broadcast Centre in Mexico City. It was set up on the table along with two microphones and some headphones, installed by a man called Stan Snape from BBC Engineering. I also had a separate telephone, red in colour, which was used at various times during the stay by Michael Grade, the controller of BBC1, the British ambassador to Mexico, the sports minister and England's third choice goalkeeper Gary Bailey, this being in the days before mobiles and laptops.

In fact, these were the days before a lot of things which have since fractured the relationships between the media and the players, fractured them to such an extent that it's now regarded as a privilege to be granted any sort of contact with even the most average of Premier League performers.

More of that later, but for now Bryon and I, along with various national newspaper journalists and TV crews were staying in the same hotel as the team. They were in another part of the complex of course. They didn't take part in our morning games of volleyball in the swimming pool, and they just waved benevolently from their dining room as David Meek from the *Manchester Evening News* and I came back from our evening run. Viv Anderson usually seemed to be by the window as we jogged gently past the security barrier. Except for the night when we passed a dead rattlesnake and legged it back pretty quickly, fearing the snake's friends and relations may have been close at hand seeking revenge.

If we wanted to speak to a player we just asked the FA press officer Glen Kirton, and he usually told us to go and sort it ourselves. It helped that the BBC Radio team consisted of just me, BB and Ron Greenwood, who was England manager before Bobby Robson took over. Bobby and Ron often talked to each other, but Ron never divulged what they were talking about and we never asked. Bobby gave us a one-on-one interview at the end of his press conferences, Bryan Robson was always happy to talk to me on behalf of the players, and for the opening game, strangely between Bulgaria and Italy, Mark Hateley agreed to pull up a chair and talk during the half-time interval.

In truth though, there was a lot of hanging about, the usual phoney war before the action began. The opening match was on May 31st and England weren't due to start until June 3rd, by which time 13 games would have already been played. On the eve of their first fixture there was even a chance that it wouldn't take place at all. Portugal were England's first opponents, and they were threatening to go on strike because of unpaid bonus money and had called a press conference in their hotel, which was just over the road from ours. We went over, BB and I, and sat around, pretty much in ignorance of what was going on, but the upshot was that the problem was solved at the last minute and on June 3rd, England lost 1-0.

The press laid into the team for being useless, Bobby Robson grew more and more morose and the pressure mounted. Surely England would still qualify for the last 16? There was only a three day gap between the Portugal game and the second match, against a Morocco team who had already taken a point in a 0-0 draw with Poland.

Robson named an unchanged line up. During the game Bryan Robson damaged his shoulder and was eventually forced to fly home, Ray Wilkins was sent off and England drew 0-0. They were almost on their way out of the competition, and when Poland beat Portugal the following day England were confirmed at the bottom of the group. Back in Saltillo it was becoming harder to persuade players to talk.

One who did agree to come and speak to us was Gary Lineker. Starved of goal scoring opportunities in the first two games, the manager had decided to give him a new striking partner for the final fixture against the Poles. Lineker would play alongside Peter Beardsley, with his Everton team-mates Trevor Steven and Peter Reid also being given starts. Gary came round to our rooms to do the interview. He'd come straight from the pool as far as I could judge, since he was wearing just a pair of shorts and flip flops. He was an interviewer's dream, articulate and intelligent, and full of confidence after scoring 30 league goals for Everton in the season just ended. With English clubs banned from Europe, this was also a rare opportunity for him to pit his wits against foreign opposition.

We talked about the game to come and about the new players in the team. Me and Gary Lineker, sat on the end of my bed in the middle of Mexico, a couple of days before both our lives changed irrevocably.

His changed because he scored a hat-trick against Poland. Mine changed when the red phone rang in my bedroom and a female voice on the other end of the line informed me I was about to become a father. My wife Alison and I had only just moved into a new house in Surrey after a year of long distance commuting into London, and now I was to "prepare for parenthood." I was thrilled and terrified at the same time, almost as terrified as the England players who had to turn out in Monterey's Universitario Stadium, knowing that they needed to win and hope.

What happened next turned many careers around. Gary Lineker scored a hat-trick and engineered a transfer to

Barcelona. Bobby Robson took England to the quarter-finals and went on to become a Knight of the Realm and a national treasure. But when the final whistle blew, I had one job to do. I had to go and interview Lineker again, provided I could find him. This time I elicited the help of Dave Bowden, BBC TV Sports' top floor manager. If you ever watched sport on TV in the latter part of the last century, Dave's face would have been familiar. He was the man in the boxing ring at the end of the big fight, or down at track side after the 100 metres final. His job was to bring the winners to the microphone to talk to the world, and he'd fight off anyone else who dared to get in his way. He was a very good man to have on your side. At the end of the game I just looked for Dave and with my tape machine on my shoulder I followed him in pursuit of England's new hero.

I don't know where we went, but it involved running round the outside of the stadium, dodging through the crowds and then fighting our way over cables and down corridors. Eventually we came to a TV studio and there, still in his football kit, was Gary Lineker. I've no idea how Dave knew he'd be there, but we crept quietly in at the back and waited. Gary was being interviewed by Mexican TV, who would ask him a question in Spanish, have it translated, and then have his answer translated back. It was the most tedious of exercises, rather like UEFA press conferences. Dave and I looked at each other, and then at our watches. We were both running short of satellite time and needed Lineker.

At last the interview ended and Dave went to organise the studio to put an earpiece on Gary so he could be spoken to by BBC TV. The Mexicans had finished with him, so as Dave went to work, Gary came over, relieved to see a friendly face. I took my chance.

"This one's in English if that's OK," I said, or something along those lines.

My first question, just three words: "Your best match?" which just opened the floodgates for the player to give his first reaction to a home audience after the performance which changed his life.

At some stage I also interviewed a delighted Bobby Robson before struggling back to the commentary position to send my material back to the International Broadcast Centre in Mexico City. My editor Derek Mitchell was on the talkback when I called in.

DEREK: "OK Pete, do we have Robson?"

ME: "Yes, and Lineker on his hat-trick."

DEREK: "Well done", which is all you needed to hear.

Before the end of the World Cup, during which Lineker scored another three goals, I interviewed him again, this time by a swimming pool in Mexico City. He was wearing the same pair of shorts and the same flip flops, and was the assured young man who'd later go on to conquer the media world.

After three years in Spain he was back in England playing for Spurs, before spending one final season in Japan with Nagoya Grampus Eight. I covered his farewell match at Elland Road in April 1993, where we spoke in the tunnel with him wearing the strange red and yellow colours of the J League side. "Siyonara Lineker san" I said in my match report. John Inverdale, who was presenting, quipped afterwards: "I knew you were going to say that, I just knew it."

Now we're all on the same side, me and John and Gary Lineker, who once sat on the edge of my bed in a Mexico hotel room. You see, I reckon he's learned much of his media know-how from those early interviews, but then I could also go onto bore you about my part in the development of Alan Shearer and Alan Hansen, and that Mark Lawrenson. But I won't. That's for another chapter.

11

Doing the Poznan, Sir Chris Hoy and the Berlin to Warsaw Express

November 2010 and Manchester City were playing in the Europa League in Poznan, a city three hours by train from the Polish capital city Warsaw. Meanwhile in one of the northern suburbs of the capital, in a place called Pruszkow, Great Britain's elite track cyclists were gathering to compete in the inaugural European Championships.

At this stage of my career, these were two events which really interested me. Since I had jumped off the Formula One treadmill in 2004, I'd been to some exotic, out of the way places in the Europa League, from rural Finland to the second largest city in Ukraine, places you'd never go to if it wasn't for the football. I'd also started following the cycling. Because of Simon Brotherton's football commitments I had been on the Tour de France four times at this stage which in turn led to doing some work in various velodromes, trying to understand the complexities of the Keirin and the Madison whilst interviewing Olympic medallists, Victoria Pendleton, Ed Clancy, Jason Kenny and, of course, Sir Chris Hoy.

So this particular week, Tracy Barwell our football organiser and I devised a plan. On Wednesday I was to fly out to Poznan with Manchester City to cover their match against Lech. On Thursday after the match, when the team flew back to Manchester, I would to stay behind, and on Friday morning, go to Poznan Railway Station to catch the Berlin to Warsaw express, which would deliver me into the capital by lunchtime. Once there I would join up with Simon Brotherton, our producer Phil Sheehan and summariser Rob Hayles before driving out to Pruzskow to cover the first evening's competition on 5 Live Sports Extra. It was my job to present the programme and interview any guests who Phil Sheehan could persuade to come up to the commentary position. Simon would do the commentary in his own inimitable way, whilst Rob, a near neighbour of mine in the Derbyshire Peak District, would add pithy comments and then come for a beer in the hotel afterwards.

The night we arrived in Poznan was typically quiet for the travelling press. It involved a mad dash across town to the stadium, the usual useless UEFA organised Roberto Mancini interview, translated from English to Polish so there was no real chance of a proper sound bite, then back to the hotel to email everything because Polish Telecom hadn't put the ISDN's in, despite it being specified on the requisition from the BBC.

We then gathered in the bar of our hotel to drink over-priced beer before heading out for dinner. This usually meant hitting the streets far too late to find anything much open. Mind you, Poznan on a wet Wednesday in November isn't quite like New York or even Manchester at the best of times. There's not a lot going on.

We eventually found a place which was willing to stay open late for us, the owner realising that he could pay the chef double and still make a profit with ten hungry journalists around. So we sat and enjoyed our meal, watching through the window as a typical pre-match night developed. It was fairly uneventful, with just a few fights, the odd group of riot police and a lot of flashing blue lights. Inside the restaurant a couple of Polish skinheads delighted in showing us their tattoos (I think they were Liverpool fans) and I was offered cocaine on my trip to the toilets. So nothing out of the ordinary as we headed back to the hotel.

The morning of the game is usually "at leisure". This means nursing the odd hangover, annoying the hotel staff by staying far too late in the breakfast room and then heading off to explore the town. Sometimes this is exciting, like in Athens when a trip to the Parthenon and the Acropolis museum is essential. In Moscow you must visit Lenin's Tomb, whilst on a visit to Finland for a match against MyPa 47, the Blackburn Rovers party toured the local town, only to find the most outstanding attraction was the Ski Jump.

In Poznan it was raining, so most people decided to stay indoors, and it was left to myself and Louise Taylor of *The Guardian* to venture out on what she always describes as "Slater Tours." Together we've explored such delights as a tower in Tallin in Estonia and the back streets of Kharkov in Ukraine, watching life pass by from a coffee shop terrace. In Poland we couldn't sit outside, the rain was too fierce, so we toured the local museum, found somewhere for elevenses and eventually went for the usual journalists late lunch, essential because it's your last chance to eat before boarding the plane home that night.

The meal was fine, the service excellent, until we came to paying the bill. Journalists always need receipts, because without receipts you can't claim your expenses. As the waitress arrived with the reckoning, I asked her if she could write on the bill that we'd had lunch, but could she write it in her native language to give the bill the authenticity we needed.

ME: "Could you write lunch in Polish please."

Waitress nod's enthusiastically.

The bill arrived, and written on the top of it were the words: "Lunch in Polish". Needless to say Louise and I tried to explain the error and I think we escaped with what we needed.

Next it was off to the game in the press bus. This is great because it always gets you through the police cordons and into the ground. If you're lucky your broadcast ISDN's are in place. If you're unlucky, like we were in Santander one December evening, they're next to the corner flag and you haven't a clue what's happening at the other end of the pitch. Sometimes they're in even more extraordinary places, like on a bus in Moscow, but that's another story entirely.

Anyway, this broadcast position was fine, and the game

started. The Poznan supporters were fantastic, producing much choreographed chanting and singing from behind the goal. When Poznan took the lead on the half hour they excelled themselves, by turning their backs on the pitch, linking arms and dancing up and down. Same thing happened when they scored again. It was a remarkable sight and the City followers obviously enjoyed it, because they've since adopted a similar routine. It's called "Doing the Poznan," and it started on that November evening in Poland.

City lost 3-1, but it didn't seem likely to spoil their chances of qualifying for the knock-out stages of this much maligned competition. Indeed these were the two sides who went through, with Lech eventually losing to Braga in the last 32, and City going out one round later to Dynamo Kiev.

After the match the press bus headed for the airport and I headed back to the hotel, where the staff superbly rustled up a late supper for myself and the ITV crew, who included commentator Clive Tyldsley and reporter Ned Boulting, who was quite envious that the following morning I was off to the cycling. Ned covers the Tour de France for ITV and we usually meet in a press compound somewhere in deepest France. One of the things we talked about was an interview I was hoping to do with Sir Chris Hoy once I reached Pruszkow. Because the Europeans were quite a low key event, there wouldn't be much media pressure on him, so with any luck he'd be able to give me ten minutes of his time for an interview which could go out across the BBC.

On the Friday morning I awoke to another gloomy Poznan day. After taking breakfast with a couple of the ITV crew I checked out. Clutching my rail ticket I took a taxi to Poznan Station, confident that I'd arrive in plenty of time to catch the 09.16 Berlin to Warsaw Express, which would whisk me eastwards in comfort. I consulted the timetable on the wall of the station to make absolutely certain that my train was scheduled to arrive when my ticket said it would, and then headed to platform two to await its arrival.

At 09.13 the Berlin to Warsaw Express arrived in Poznan

Station. Unfortunately for me it pulled into platform one, which was across the tracks from where I was standing. I knew it was the Berlin to Warsaw Express because it had those very words written on its side. Blind panic ensued as I tried to work out what to do. First of all I needed to make certain that that was indeed the train that I wanted. I waved my ticket in front of a middle aged Polish woman who was standing next to me, pointing at it and at the train. She nodded in agreement, confirming my worst fears. I was about to miss the train, which would mean I'd miss the crew in Warsaw and probably miss the first nights programme. I'd certainly miss the chance to interview Sir Chris Hoy.

This called for decisive action as I picked up my luggage and my ISDN kit and raced along the platform, down the steps and under the track, up the other side and onto platform one. I clambered aboard just in time to hear the guard's whistle blow, and we were off to Warsaw.

Tracy had booked me a seat, but I looked in vain for the right carriage number before finding a spare place in another compartment. This train was like the ones we used to have in the UK, with a corridor down one side and compartments with six seats in each, three people facing each other.

I settled down to read my book, which was *The White Tiger* by Aravind Adiga, the winner of The Booker Prize in 2008. It was all about a young entrepreneur in India and I became quite absorbed in it as the train thundered on through the Polish countryside. Occasionally I looked around at my travelling companions, who were avidly reading their morning papers. I could see the headlines on the sports pages, mainly about Lech Poznan's fine 3-1 win over Manchester City the night before.

After about half an hour a thought struck me. I was travelling on the Berlin to Warsaw Express, and yet all the other travellers were reading Polish Newspapers. That wasn't odd in itself, except that surely, if this train had come from Berlin, someone would be reading Bild, or Allemagne Zeitung. No one was.

A sinking feeling ran through me. I was normally a very

efficient traveller, quite happy to organise my own transport wherever I went. I walked out into the corridor and saw the route plan stuck to the window. Sure enough, I was on the Berlin to Warsaw Express, but it was going from Warsaw to Berlin. I was on the right train but heading in the wrong direction.

At that moment the ticket collector came along. She was a very pleasant young lady and she spoke English. She spoke it well enough to inform me through her badly disguised smirk, that the train I should have been on had arrived in Poznan two minutes after the one I was on had left. She then told me that I would have to leave this train at the next station stop and wait for the next express to come through from Berlin. Unfortunately our train didn't stop for another 45 minutes, by which time we'd have reached Rzepin, close to the German border. This was where I had to disembark and wait for my connection.

I called Phil Sheehan and explained what had happened. He promised that the crew wouldn't take the mickey, at least not for the entire weekend, and said that as long as I could make the arena by 20.00 hours I'd be fine, since Sports Extra had decided they weren't going to do the whole programme from Pruszkow that night, although I'd be required to do interviews after the first final, the Women's Team Pursuit, which started at 20.15. As for Sir Chris Hoy, we could sort that out for the following morning, when he was due to take part in the preliminary rounds of the Men's Sprint.

The train continued its inexorable journey towards Germany. Eventually, in the late morning of a November Friday, it slowed down and pulled into Rzepin.

Now I don't know how many of you have ever been to Rzepin, but there's not a lot to see. For a start the station is quite a long way out of town, so it's rather like Rzepin Parkway. It was there, however, that I had my first stroke of luck that day. The lady in the ticket office, who tried hard to hide her laughs as I explained that I needed a ticket from Rzepin to Poznan, even though I'd just come off a train from Poznan, took pity on this ridiculous foreigner and allowed me to leave my luggage in her office. This was very kind of her, her kindness partly explained when I looked at the rather rudimentary timetable (It wasn't that extensive, not many trains stopped at Rzepin). The next train for Warsaw, stopping first at Poznan, wasn't for another three and a half hours.

So I headed off to explore the delights of the town, with the November wind blowing across the plains. I comforted myself with the fact that at least it wasn't raining and I had enough Polish zlotys to keep body and soul together. Unfortunately I didn't have Louise Taylor with me otherwise we could have made this a Slater Tour to remember. I walked past a rather sad looking kiosk, which was closed, and headed off in the direction of the town. I passed some Polish workers who were mending the road, then a tanning salon and something which looked like the local co-op. It was late in the morning and I thought I'd find somewhere to have a cup of coffee and watch the world go by. I passed another tanning salon and then the only hotel in town, which appeared to be closed.

At last I spotted what looked like a restaurant. It was called Mak, and was next to a tanning salon and opposite a hairdressers. The owner, a young man in a leather jacket, was putting out a sign advertising coffee. This looked promising, so I went in and ordered a cup. This was brought to me by a young lady, who was also putting out menus for lunch. The menu was entirely in Polish. There was zupy, pierogia a'lamak, and dania glowne, none of which made the slightest bit of sense to someone who, by now, should have been heading off to the velodrome in Warsaw.

I sat and sipped my coffee, reading my book and then glancing at the menu. Should I have the sandacz grilowany for 26 zloty, or splash out on kurczaki w ciescie for 40 zloty? What I really wanted was chicken and chips, and there was only one way to make sure that was what I ordered.

As the waitress approached, I flapped my arms like a chicken and made clucking noises. She seemed to understand, and about twenty minutes later came back with a very acceptable lunch.

After that it was just a question of walking back to Rzepin Station, past the Co-op, the road menders and the tanning salon and the closed down hotel with the wind whistling across the flat lands of western Poland. I was going to make absolutely certain of catching the train this time, and sure enough, around five hours after I boarded it for the first time, in came the Berlin to Warsaw Express, this time travelling in the right direction. I knew it was travelling towards the Polish capital, because who should be there to greet me but the very same ticket collector who'd ushered me from the train three and a half hours earlier. She was still trying hard to disguise her smirk.

Within ninety minutes I was back in Poznan, sitting in the train on platform two, well aware that if I'd waited just another couple of minutes that morning the train I needed to catch would have come through, and by now I'd be sitting down at the velodrome, pre-recording the various interviews we needed with our top track cyclists, amongst them Sir Chris Hoy.

At this point I should mention that I'd interviewed Chris a few times before and always found him very approachable. Now, of course, he was a Knight of the Realm, BBC Sports Personality of the Year and an ambassador for a well know brand of breakfast cereal. But with so few other media around this could prove to be the best interview so far.

By now the rest of the crew, Simon, Phil and Rob, would be setting up the OB, putting together the running orders, and chuckling about the idiot abroad who'd managed to make a mess of the simplest of travel arrangements. I'd been left to fend for myself once I arrived in Warsaw. All I knew was that there was a small, suburban railway station in Pruszkow, and that if I made it that far then a rescue party could come out and find me.

I sat in my compartment watching the darkness settle over Poland, wondering how I was going to find my way to the track. My travelling companions were engrossed in either texting reading or sleeping. No-one was talking, until my friend the collector came in to check the tickets and asked me, in English, how I'd enjoyed my stay in Rzepin. I then discovered that of the remaining four people in the compartment, one was Swedish, one came from Nigeria and a third, who was Polish, spoke good English. It was explained to me, after they'd stopped laughing, that to reach Pruskow I needed to transfer onto something called the "Vookoda," whatever that was. "Just ask" was the suggestion.

At around 18.00 hours we arrived at Warsaw Central Station and I set off to look for this mysterious "Vookoda." I then spotted a sign which said WKD, and the real traveller in me realised that I'd been given the phonetic spelling for the suburban line I needed. On I trundled, past the flower stalls and refreshment kiosks, bumping into rush hour commuters desperate to get home for the weekend.

At last, at the far end of the station I found the small platform for the WKD. I purchased a ticket for Pruszkow, making sure to pronounce it as my travelling companion had told me, "Prush-kov-a". At last I felt I was back on track as I punched the ticket on the machine inside the carriage, and sat down to wait for the train to move. Then two things happened. First of all there was an announcement in Polish which I didn't understand. Then a group of youths told me that I shouldn't have punched the ticket, because, and here I paraphrase their halting English, it was timed from the moment I validated it, and the train wasn't moving since someone had thrown themselves in front of a previous train and we were stuck in this siding at the far end of Warsaw Central.

After what seemed like ages but which was probably no more than another half an hour, the train started to move. We were on our way to Pruszkow. I could follow our progress on the map which was posted just above the exit doors, or at least I could have done but the stations we went through, in what was now stygian blackness, had hardly any lighting, let alone signs to indicate where we actually were. It was now after 19.00 and I was getting desperate. Would I even be there for the first final of the evening?

Then there was another stroke of luck. The mobile of the woman opposite me rang and she started to conduct a conversation in English. When she finished I asked her if she could identify the stations for me, since I was finding it difficult to see any signage, and furthermore the windows were misting up. She told me that Pruszkow was her final destination, and that she'd also be able to show me where the velodrome was when we arrived.

So at around 19.40 hours, nearly seven hours late, I got off the WKD train and headed off through a housing estate to find what I'd been reliably informed was the venue for the European Track Cycling Championships. As I rounded a corner I saw it shining in front of me, like a beacon of light at the top of a hill. As I trundled my luggage towards the entrance I saw Dave Brailsford, British Cycling's performance director, in the middle of a rather animated telephone call. He waved a hand in acknowledgement as Phil Sheehan came out of the building, smiling broadly, with my accreditation in his hand.

As we entered the building I just had time to give him my ISDN kit, extricate my recording equipment and stand and watch as the Women's Pursuit team won the gold medal. Within ten minutes of arriving I was in the centre of the track interviewing Wendy Houvenaghel and the rest of the squad. If only they'd known what sort of a day I'd had, but then why would they?

The rest of the evening passed uneventfully. I conducted several interviews ready for Saturdays show, and apart from an altercation with a Polish traffic policeman who accused me of jay walking, I finished the night in one of Warsaw's top hotels, with a view of the Presidential Palace and a souvenir, from the Mak Restauracja in Rzepin, where the waitress was probably still telling the locals about the strange man who did chicken impersonations. I knew that Saturday would be a big day, because I had to go and interview Sir Chris Hoy

Saturday dawned cold but bright in Warsaw. I enjoyed breakfast and crossed the square to meet the others at their hotel ready for the drive out to Pruszkow. This time it was far more straightforward and we arrived within about 45 minutes of leaving, despite taking a wrong turning close to a giant poster of the Polish Formula One racing driver Robert Kubicka.

We'd taken a decision the previous evening to skip the early rounds of the Men's Sprint, mainly because it was likely to be deadly dull with Chris Hoy and the other leading contenders passing easily into the quarter finals. In fact the velodrome was half empty and down in the press seats the only familiar face was William Fotheringham, cycling correspondent of *The Guardian*, and a good friend of BBC Radio Sport.

WILLIAM: "Good of you lot to show up. Haven't you heard what's happened? "

US: "No, go on, surprise us."

WILLIAM: "Chris Hoy's been knocked out. He's packed his bags and he's on his way to the airport."

It was a classic Fotheringham wind up, it had to be. Chris Hoy was the top seed. He'd been drawn against an 18-year-old named Felix English, who was riding for Ireland and who would have been ecstatic simply to have been on the same track as the great man.

US: "Pull the other one William, now where's the coffee?"

William continued to protest that he was telling us the truth, and as we looked around the centre of the track there was no sign of Hoy, or of his coaches. Surely this most unlikely of sporting events couldn't have happened? In fact, please let it not have happened because we'd missed it! For the second time in 24 hours I had that sinking feeling, just like I'd had on the train the previous morning.

But it had happened. A former English youth cyclist, who'd joined the Irish team because Chris Hoy's form would never have allowed him a chance of making the senior squad, had knocked the World and Olympic Champion out in the round of the last 16.

It transpired that Chris Hoy had led his opponent out, and on the last lap, when he normally accelerated to the line, Hoy had simply coasted round because he was so far ahead of his opponent. It was almost as if he didn't want to embarrass the poor lad by beating him convincingly. Young Felix just put his head down and started closing the gap. Chris Hoy simply didn't look behind him, and when Felix rushed past him just before the line there was nothing he could do.

So instead of interviewing Chris Hoy about his hopes for the coming two years, about the build-up to the Olympic Games and the way his life had changed since Beijing and all that, I was off on another chase, to find Felix English, the 18-year-old from Brighton, who'd decided to ride for the country of his parents, and who was only in the sprint "for experience."

At the bottom of the stairs, underneath the track centre in suburban Warsaw I did indeed conduct the major interview of the day, an interview which sparked interest around the cycling world. But it wasn't with Sir Chris Hoy, it was with a delighted young man in a green shirt. As for the Olympic Champion, he'd been heading for the finish line, but somehow something had gone wrong. Happens to us all Chris, happens to us all.

12

Wembley – Venue of Embarrassment and Humiliation

In another part of this book I'll talk about my experiences of working at the "new" Wembley, with its state of the art facilities and co-operative staff, a stadium built with the media of the 21st century in mind. That chapter will also involve some swearing live on air and trying to find anyone I could recognise on the pitch after the football world's gone mad. It's a chapter about the play-offs, about Billy and Ollie, about Deano and Adie, about ecstasy and agony in the same place at the same time. It's also about Gary Neville, but as I said, that comes later.

This is about the old stadium, the Twin Towers, a concrete edifice built in the wrong part of London, where thousands would descend every so often for cup finals and internationals. It was difficult to reach, almost impossible to escape from, and the working conditions weren't helped by "jobsworths," who conspired to stop you doing what you were being paid to do. Despite all that Wembley's provided me with plenty of delightful memories, and some very good interviews.

It was at Wembley where I had a close encounter with Diego Maradona. Where Middlesbrough goalkeeper Mark Schwarzer showed that footballers can have a sense of humour, and where I interviewed Eric Cantona, twice. It was also at Wembley where I wrongly identified a cup winning Manager, was blanked by one of the most reliable interviewees in the game, and was thrown off the pitch during a live broadcast by an over officious steward.

I'll start with Coventry City, because after that things can only improve. It was May 16th 1987, and the Sky Blues had reached their first ever FA Cup Final. They were managed by an impressive double act, George Curtis and John Sillett, and were up against Tottenham Hotspur, a team which included Ray Clemence in goal, Waddle and Hoddle in midfield, Clive Allen up front, and Ossie Ardiles, going to Wembley with his "knees all trembly."

At that time I was BBC Radio's football producer and after organising the coverage for both domestic and foreign broadcasters, I was to sort out and conduct pre-match and post-match interviews. Before the game this meant pulling players across to speak as they went out onto the pitch and tested the grass, waved to their families and posed in their cup final suits. Working alongside me was Jeff Stelling, someone I'd known from my days in the North-East, and who was now working for BBC Radio before moving on to become a Saturday afternoon legend on Sky Sports.

We conducted a number of interviews between us. Tottenham's manager at the time was David Pleat, who was also one of my regular summarisers, and the Coventry boys were just so pleased to be part of the occasion. We were allowed to interview on the pitch apron, a sanded area behind the goal, and we had no shortage of takers. When the game kicked off we retreated to the radio commentary box, which was high under the rafters on the Wembley roof. It was an area beyond the reach of the general public, and allowed us privileges they would have paid a fortune to experience. I've taken my packed lunch up there and sat leaning against one of the actual twin towers in the late spring sunshine. During most cup finals, we'd watch from high amongst the girders, usually with John the air conditioning supervisor, far away from the security checks and the maddening crowd down below.

As this particular game drew to a close, Jeff and I were due to make our way down the stairs, through the famous Long Bar and into the tunnel. There were several security checks along the way, but the doormen usually recognised us and allowed us through. The scores were level this year, but you couldn't rely on extra time, because someone was always likely to fashion a winner in the final minutes, at which point you'd be in completely the wrong place and faced with a ten minute walk as the crowd tried to leave. I've watched extra time on a number of occasions from the top of the tunnel, trying to spot what's going on through a mass of bodies. It's virtually impossible.

On May 16th 1987, Coventry City beat Tottenham 3-2 after extra time. For the reporting team down near the pitch this meant that time was of the essence. The Saturday programme had to come off air at six o'clock and we'd already lost half an hour because of the additional playing time. In those days, even BBC TV and ITV were limited to how much time they were allowed on the pitch. BBC Radio weren't allowed on it at all. Normally I'd wait at our fixed broadcast point halfway down the tunnel, listening to Peter Jones describing the presentation ceremony, and listening to the roar of the crowd which would either be deafening or distant, depending on which end of the ground the victorious supporters were based.

Then you had to try and stop the winning manager and players and speak to them. We used a fixed microphone, because down in the tunnel the radio mics wouldn't work. If you wanted to use them you had to break cover at the top of the tunnel and to do that meant stepping over a line which the Wembley security didn't want you to.

Time was running out that Saturday afternoon. Brian Kilcline had limped up to collect the Cup, Curtis and Sillett were dancing on the running track, and the whole of Coventry was celebrating. We hadn't had an interview and the clock was moving towards 6.00pm. It required drastic action.

So I moved up the tunnel to pitch level and picked up the radio mic. The studio producer was asking for a Coventry interview, any Coventry interview. If the man who drove the team bus had appeared at that stage we'd have spoken to him. The problem was that the players were all at the far end of the stadium, and security were making sure that we didn't go anywhere near them.

Then out of the corner of my eye I saw the giant, bearded figure of Brian Kilcline. He was limping towards the dressing rooms, and he was clutching the FA Cup in his hands. An interview then would make a perfect radio moment, the captain of the side, holding the cup on the Wembley turf at his moment of greatest triumph. However, in order to reach him I had to step off the sanded perimeter and stand on the pitch. So I moved forward, attracted Brian's attention and called the producer, who had me on pre-fade in his little studio in the bowels of the stadium. "Come to me now, I have Brian Kilcline for interview" I said, or words to that effect. The studio were so grateful that we'd managed to find someone at last that they cued straight over. What followed was a moment of excruciating embarrassment, both for myself and for the Coventry City captain.

The radio log would have sounded something like this.

PRESENTER: "Now we can go down to pitch side, where Peter Slater is ready to speak to one of the Coventry players."

ME: "Yes, thank you, I'm here with the Sky Blues skipper Brian Kilcline, and he's holding the FA Cup in his hands. Brian just how special an afternoon is this for you and for the club."

The next voice you heard was supposed to be Brian's. Instead it was an angry steward, saying live on air, "You've been told you're not to come onto the pitch to do interviews so get off now."

I think I managed to hand back to the studio, apologise to Kilcline and maybe even remonstrate with the official who'd physically separated me from my interviewee. It was not my finest broadcasting moment.

Worse was to follow. I retreated to the fixed microphone, and as George Curtis and John Sillett came down the tunnel I was able to stop them for interview. This time the stewards couldn't stop me because I was within the required zone. We talked for a couple of minutes and things seemed to be going well. Then my producer told me to wind up, probably because we had to get off air and hand over to the next programme.

So I started to finish the interview, at the end of which I looked at Sillett and said, "thank you and congratulations George." To which he replied, quite deadpan, "Thank you and I'm John."

My two big moments and I'd been thrown off the pitch and then called the manager by his colleague's name. I was mortified and miserable as I made my way back across town to the Dover Castle pub, close by Broadcasting House, where we used to meet post-cup final for a drink. I'd made two terrible errors and was ready to be chastised by my editor. Of course, nobody else had noticed a thing, all they were concerned about was that the programme had now been put to bed and summer had arrived.

What it did teach me was to keep your head under pressure and to obey the rules, because even if you don't like them, they're there to be observed. Nowadays I am allowed onto the pitch to interview managers and players, it's almost expected, and I'll detail that elsewhere. But what I didn't know on May 16th 1987 was that during the afternoon our match summariser and our special guest had been having a long chat up in the commentary box. One was Don Howe and the other Bobby Gould, and twelve months later they'd be back at Wembley, plotting one of the greatest FA Cup Final upsets of all time. Because on that afternoon, as my broadcasting world was falling down around my ears, Gould asked Howe to come and join him at Wimbledon, and in May 1988 Wimbledon beat Liverpool to win the cup.

Down in the tunnel after that game I interviewed Bobby and Don, and this time made absolutely certain I had both their names correct. You see, learning all the time from mistakes.

13

Eric Cantona Says "Oui", Steve Bruce Says "No"

I first tried to interview Eric Cantona some time in 1992. He was playing for Leeds United and had just scored a couple of goals in a game at Boundary Park in Oldham. He didn't speak much English, so I used my friendship with the Leeds United striker Lee Chapman in order to conduct a not particularly successful conversation at the side of the pitch.

Lee was a regular contributor to BBC Radio Sport at that time. I'd identified him as a bright, articulate footballer, and we used him to host a regular slot on Saturday afternoons, when he'd link up with a couple of other footballers to discuss the events of the week. I'd normally drive up to Elland Road on a Friday morning to record this feature, which would be linked through our London studios.

Lee also spoke a bit of French, partly due to his unsuccessful stay with the French club Niort. In fact, in the early autumn of 1988, Mike Ingham and I had travelled to France to interview some of the English players who'd decided to make the break and go and play across the Channel. We took tea with Clive Allen in Bordeaux, met Brian Stein at a rehab centre in Brittany, and enjoyed café life with Graham Rix in Caen. However by the time we reached Niort to speak to Chapman, he'd fallen out with the club and returned home, where he was to crown his career by collecting a Championship Winners medal for Leeds United in the last season before the Premier League took over.

So Lee Chapman was acting as Eric Cantona's interpreter

and we tried to conduct this bizarre interview, with me asking questions, Lee translating, Eric answering and so forth. Needless to say it didn't work, and before I had the chance to talk with the enigmatic Frenchman again he'd moved across the Pennines to Old Trafford, where he went on to become a Manchester United legend.

For whatever reason, once he arrived in Manchester, Cantona stopped doing interviews. Whenever you came across him, in mixed zones or at the training ground, he simply walked straight past. However this wasn't of great concern because at that time United possessed a number of players who were both good and reliable talkers, players who'd always stop for a chat. The best of the lot was Steve Bruce, often the captain of the team and destined to become a popular and successful manager.

Bruce was captain when United beat Chelsea 4-0 in 1994, a match where Cantona scored twice from the penalty spot. As with Coventry City in 1987, my job was to work in the tunnel, trying to interview as many of the winning team as possible. It's an area called, quite rightly, The Bear Pit, because after the game the place is awash with TV crews, officials, players, stewards and general hangers on. You have to fight for everything and as Eric Cantona approached I thought, "why not," and asked him if he could spare me a couple of minutes for an interview. I expected him to walk on by, but on this occasion he didn't. The enigmatic Frenchman stopped. Excitedly I shouted to my producer: "Cross now, you won't believe who I have with me." So they crossed over and, rather proudly, I announced; "Joining us here live on BBC Radio is Eric Cantona."

Now you have to remember that whilst Eric's English had improved by then, it wasn't brilliant, so I had to make sure my questions were simple and precise. Trouble was, that as the conversation, such as it was, developed, I ended up sounding less and less like a BBC interviewer and more and more like Inspector Clouseau. Still, what did I care, I'd managed to interview the great Eric Cantona, and the studio was delighted.

By now I was feeling pretty good about things, and also rather too confident for my own good. As Cantona made his way towards the dressing rooms, I looked up the steps leading from the TV studio and spotted Steve Bruce. He was walking down the stairs, with the FA Cup in his hands. I didn't need to ask if he'd stop to talk to me, because I knew that Steve always did. So I called the studio and told them to cue over straight away as I had Steve Bruce available for interview.

The presenter handed over at the precise moment that Steve Bruce walked by, saying "Can't stop, I've got to take the cup into the dressing room." He headed off down the tunnel, leaving me with an open microphone and no interviewee. I was struck dumb, literally not knowing what to say. So I kept quiet as the producer shouted down the talk back line, "Go Peter". After a couple of seconds the presenter said, "We don't seem to be able to hear from Peter at the moment, we'll go back to him later." I then told the studio that I'd lost cue for a few seconds, something about a headphone socket being dislodged, and eventually Steve Bruce did re-appear and I was able to interview him.

A couple of years later United won the FA Cup again, beating Liverpool 1-0. Cantona was still in the team but Steve Bruce had moved on. With no such thing as a press officer to help or hinder, it was still a case of fending for yourself down in the tunnel. Of course I wanted to interview Cantona again, but he wasn't talking, although I had mentioned to Ken Ramsden, United's assistant secretary, that if the player changed his mind, I'd be interested.

Halfway down the Wembley tunnel, on the opposite side to the dressing rooms, was a small room, no bigger than a cupboard really. I was never sure what went on in there, but occasionally you could use it as an improvised interview room. I was hanging around waiting for instructions from the studio, with the programme about to go off air, when Ned Kelly, Manchester United's head of security, called me over.

"You're Radio 5 Live aren't you?" he asked. I nodded, "Come with me then," and since Ned was ex SAS, you didn't argue with him.

He took me across to the cupboard, and there inside, bare chested and completely alone, was Eric Cantona. I remember he had a tattoo of what looked like an eagle on his chest.

Now it was too late to do a live interview, but fortunately one of our sound engineers was in the vicinity, carrying with him a portable tape machine, just in case we managed to find a suitable person to talk to. Believe me when I say that no-one was more suitable than Cantona. So we stood in the cupboard and talked for around five minutes, about the game and about his hopes for future seasons. I couldn't believe my luck. For some reason we'd been granted an exclusive. Perhaps it was down to my friendship with Ken Ramsden, who I'd helped out at a Silverstone Grand Prix once, sorting out lunch for him in the paddock. Now he had returned the favour.

The interview finished, we raced back to the control room, where they played it into David Mellor's 6-0-6 programme. Mellor cued it by saying, "We don't often hear from Eric Cantona, so we're interrupting the phone-in to do just that."

It was a proud moment indeed for your BBC interviewer, and proved that it wasn't always a disaster working in the old stadium, just very hard work sometimes. As for Eric, that was the last time, to date at least, that we've spoken. He did turn up at a Formula One race one weekend, but seemed disinclined to speak, even on the grid, where only the really rich and famous are allowed. Which takes me off in another direction entirely.

Metro Radio publicity photo 1976. With Charles Harrison, the man who gave me my first chance as a professional broadcaster

Brendon Foster's athletics events at Gateshead gave me the chance to interview many of the world's top competitors. Here I'm with top 400 metre runner the late Donna Hartley, waiting for Charles to cue me in by the looks of it

Henry Rono broke four world records in 1978. At Gateshead in September he finished second to Sebastian Coe in the mile race

I had many happy days covering speedway. Here I am sitting on the podium in the pits at the 1983 World Final in Norden, West Germany – a bit like holding the event in Thurso!

When I joined the BBC I was given a number of sports to produce. Here I'm at Hickstead covering the British Jumping Derby with Peter Churchill

World Cup, Mexico 1986
My first major foreign assignment for the BBC

In the gardens of the England team hotel, Saltillo, with Bryon Butler on my right and Ron Greenwood on my left

Bobby Robson prepares to go live from my hotel bathroom, Mexico City 1986. Bryon Butler in the foreground. My career wouldn't have been so successful without Bob

I first met Terry Butcher when I was at Ipswich. He later worked for BBC Sport as a summariser. Here we are after an England training session

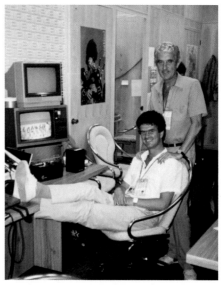

At the International Broadcast Centre in Mexico City with legendary commentator Peter Jones. Sadly Peter died too young at just 60 years of age

By the England team bus, Euro 88, a forgettable tournament for the national team

Olympic Stadium, Rome, with John Inverdale, who still comes out to the Peak District, mainly to talk about Steely Dan

Italia 90, looking in control as BBC Radio's studio producer for the 1990 World Cup

Hanging around with Kevin Keegan at St James' Park in the early 1990s as he conducts an interview for *Sports Report*,

Before the embarrasment at the 1987 FA Cup Final. Messing about on the pitch
pre-match with Trevor Brooking, Jeff Stelling and Ron Jones

Two visits to Mosow within three weeks of each other. Wearing a
Russian hat and with Jimmy Armfield, probably the most respected
man in football (him, not me!)

Our first F1 season. With Jonathan Legard in Monaco, May 1997. We worked together for eight seasons – he's a top pro

Safari Rally March 1994. Carnivores Restaurant Nairobi. No Idea what I'm being served!

Interviewing Anthony Davidson on the F1 grid, Budapest 2002. ITV's Louise Goodman listens in with interest while top F1 photographer Mark Thompson looks for the best picture

Ross Brawn accepts the E.I.Addio Trophy, Becketts Bar, Budapest August 2003. The BBC's current F1 correspondent, James Allan, is on the extreme left with his arm around Jean Brawn. Kevin Garside is giving it the thumbs down, Jim Rosenthal and Jonathan Legard look excited over on the right

By the last race in the season in Japan, only the hardcore reporters were left. From left to right: Kevin Eason (*The Times*), Ian Gordon (Press Association), Ray Matts (*Daily Mail*), Jason Swales (BBC producer), Stan Peicha (*The Sun*), Bob McKenzie (*Daily Express*), Steve Cooper (*Motorsport News*), Byron Young (*Daily Mirror*), me, Jon Noble (*Autosport*) and Maurice Hamilton (*Observer* and BBC Radio summariser)

So we put the microphone next to the air conditioner and it did indeed sound like a helicopter. BBC Radio's Tour de France team, L'Alpe d'Huez 2010. Phil Sheehan on my right, Graham Jones on my left
Photo: Andy Jones, *Cycling Weekly*

And you are? Mark Cavendish ignores top BBC reporter. Tour of Britain, Blackpool, September 2012

Some of the crew en route to the Rio International Broadcast Centre, posing in front of the Olympic Park. TJ Jeffrey, my wonderful picture editor, is seated on my immediate left

Segment reporters at the end of their 29 day stint. Among them are well-known broadcasting voices including Delyth Lloyd, Mike Sewell and Lynsey Hooper. I'm in the middle of the back row, Richard Askam, my Rio flat mate, is on the front row at the far right

14

Who's That Behind Martin Brundle?

Some magazine article, presumably one financed by someone to do with motor racing, once declared that the Formula One paddock in the hours before a race is the most glamorous place in the world to be. That's not necessarily the case if you're at Spa and it's raining, or if the wind's whistling across the Northamptonshire plains and straight down the Start-Finish Straight at Silverstone.

It can't be denied though that in the hours leading up to the race there's an awful lot of posing going on in the paddock, as the lunch tables are set and the drivers prepare. There's the Paddock Club, where normally sane business people pay a small fortune for the chance to meet an overalled member of an F1 team or maybe go on a visit to the garage, where they can gaze on a real life Formula One car. For the elite, each team is allowed a certain number of guest passes to take the very special VIP's onto the grid, and when you're a pit lane reporter with a radio microphone and a pass which allows you there as well, your job is to try and grab as many of the famous as possible to speak to you.

One year the producer just gave me complete licence to "Do a Martin Brundle," in other words just walk and talk with whoever I could find. That's OK if you can square it with the teams' media staff to speak to their drivers (who, amazingly, talk just before hurtling off down the track) and also if you can find the odd team principal who's happy to chat. Otherwise you could be left talking to yourself, but in my day there were usually plenty of volunteers. We had characters like team owner Eddie Jordan, Patrick Head, part owner of Williams, McLaren's CEO Ron Dennis and Ross Brawn, technical director at Ferrari. Further down the grid Minardi owner Paul Stoddart would always speak, as would Sir Jackie Stewart, one of those I'd mark down as the best interviewee of all time.

The British drivers were usually happy to talk to me. David Coulthard is a gentleman, Eddie Irvine and Johnny Herbert would pass the time of day, Jenson Button was OK provided you'd organised it with him before hand, and the lesser known men like Anthony Davidson and Justin Wilson were just happy for the publicity.

Like I said, on the grid were the very rich, the moderately famous, and the journalists, who'd wander on under the pretext of examining the cars, but who often wanted just to appear in the back of shot when the aforementioned Brundle was doing his famous grid walk for television. Watching from the comfort of your armchairs you'd see these guys on their mobile phones and think that they were passing on information to their editors about what they'd seen. What in fact they were doing were calling their friends at home to say; "Martin's coming along, and you can see me in the back of his shot. I'm actually speaking to you as you watch." I'm amazed they didn't wave as well, in fact some of them probably did!

The past master of all this was Kevin Garside of the *Daily Telegraph*. He'd constantly show up just as Brundle was about to talk to some fading film star or other. My son even had a tee-shirt made of various Garside TV moments, and brought it to a race with a "Wanted, Have You Seen This Man?" sign on the top. It was very funny, and Kevin took it in the spirit in which it was meant, which was that he should just stop posing and get on with doing his job.

So who have I stopped to speak to on the F1 grid, as they wandered wide-eyed between the cars? Well certainly not the Brazilian soap star who was surrounded by local crews but who was unknown to anyone else. I didn't approach the man at the A1 Ring who was dressed in lederhosen, to discover that he was in fact "The Most Famous Weather Presenter in Austria." I avoided Nicholas Cage in Montreal, mainly because Nicholas Cage was deliberately avoiding everyone by wearing dark glasses and surrounding himself with security men. The price of fame indeed.

One person I did speak to in Canada, and I use the word loosely, was one John Michael Osbourne, one time lead singer with Black Sabbath, latterly a reality TV star and oft impersonated almost national treasure.

Ozzie had been performing in Montreal the previous evening, and from the way he was wandering about the grid looked like his mind was still on the stage somewhere. Undeterred I told the studio, who always kept me on pre-fade during the half hour leading up to the race, to stand by to record. I wasn't going to chance going live with Osbourne, because you'd never be too sure what he would come out with. I have had interviewees swear live on air, as detailed elsewhere in this book, but I was taking no risks here.

I asked Ozzie's minder if the great man would mind speaking to the BBC for a couple of minutes. Always worked, the BBC, like he thought he'd be communicating with the folks back home. As it turned out, he was hardly capable of communicating at all. I tried, believe me I tried. I asked him about his interest in F1 (there didn't appear to be much), I asked him how the concert had gone (he didn't seem to know) and about his plans for the rest of the year (he was pretty vague). All in all I think we spoke for about 90 seconds, and the studio edited it down to about half that. It was one of those occasions when you can tell people that you'd interviewed a rock legend, but this time it was hardly worth the bother. The programme ran it though!

Other musicians have faced the Slater microphone with slightly better results; some love their football, others like their cars. Some, like Phil Collins, I've met twice, once in the board room at Tottenham and once in the Stewart motorhome at a Grand Prix. There are footballers who've turned up at Grands Prix, and racing drivers who've pretended to be interested in football (was Johnny Herbert really a Chelsea fan?)

Back on the F1 grid, there was an incident with Sol Campbell, when he was about to move clubs. I can't remember whether he was moving from Spurs to Arsenal or going somewhere else. All I do recall is that a) he was wearing the most ridiculous pair of flowery shorts I've ever seen, and b) he wasn't talking to anyone about anything. Not that anyone else wanted to speak to him. To the rest of the world he was about as exciting as Austria's Best Known Weather Man.

I suppose I should mention Pele at this juncture, although he wasn't actually on the F1 grid. I was offered the chance to talk to him by the harbour in Monte Carlo, where he was a guest of one of the teams. I think he was a friend of Rubens Barrichello, who in turn was one of the more approachable F1 drivers. We talked about his role as a football ambassador for a major credit card company, and about his charity work, and whilst it was a thrill to meet the great man again (I'd been stood next to Bryon Butler when he'd interviewed Pele on the pitch at Wembley before an FA centenary game) I can't recall it being one of my more memorable encounters.

I bumped into Jeremy Clarkson on the grid in Monaco, and we passed a pleasant 60 seconds. Snooker player Stephen Hendrie turned up a couple of times, and we talked about his yellow Ferrari and love of fast cars. The great thing about Hendrie was that none of the other media crews knew who he was and Martin Brundle and I had him to ourselves. The same thing happened with England World Cup Rugby winner Matt Dawson, who could walk unmolested amongst the cars. Matt was happy to talk and as those who listen to Radio 5 Live can vouch, he hasn't stopped much since he finished playing.

The superstars were harder to nail of course. Arnold Schwarzenegger arrived one day at Silverstone, and although I tried to get near him, it proved impossible. In fact, we did broadcast one amusing moment when I was describing the moving scrum around the strangely hued governor of California (he's orange you know!) alongside the singer and musician Chris de Burgh, who'd just returned from a tour of Russia, where he'd rejoiced in saying the words, "Good evening Nizgy Novgorod!"

The conversation in the pit lane and on the grid was usually centred around the celebrities' impressions of F1 and the cars, maybe what sort of vehicles they drove at home, and what other sports they enjoyed. It was a successful formula, because for once these people were outside their normal sphere of experience, and happy to stop droning on about their latest film/album/tour.

As well as entertainment royalty we've also had genuine royalty on the grid. King Juan Carlos of Spain was a regular visitor to the Circuit de Catalunya for the Spanish Grand Prix. I interviewed the Crown Prince of Bahrain, a man educated in Britain and someone with a great interest in British football. I think I offered him a job reporting on lower league games for the BBC. I once walked past Princess Diana at Silverstone and swore she gave me a flirtatious look, but then I'm almost certainly imagining it.

As the magazine writer claimed, there is something glamorous about the paddock and pit lane on the day of an F1 race. For those of us who've been privileged to experience it week in week out for eight seasons it possibly loses its appeal, simply becoming a place of work. You might be talking to Boris Becker one week and Michael Owen the next. You may have time to speak to delightful people like Irish rugby captain Keith Wood or TV chef Gary Rhodes, both of whom filled in the interminable minutes on qualifying Saturday, when we had the air time but nothing to commentate on.

Since this chapter is about those who tried to appear behind Martin Brundle, I can't let it pass without mentioning the man himself, the garage proprietor from Kings Lynn who went on to drive for several Formula One teams and then moved seamlessly into the commentary box.

As you would expect, given the path his career eventually followed, Brundle was always easy to interview. It helped me that when he was at Jordan his race engineer was Andy Tilley, who I'd first met with Mika Hakkinen back in France in 1992.

Together they helped me put together a feature about the team behind the team, which we used at the British Grand Prix in 1996. It was the sort of thing which eventually helped land me the pit lane reporters Job, and I'm very grateful to both of them for their co-operation.

By the following year, both Martin and I found ourselves in Melbourne with new challenges. I was 5 Live's new boy in the pit lane, Martin had crossed over to become ITV's race summariser, a job he took to like a duck to water. No-one in the media was surprised. However, because he was working for "The Other Side," I couldn't interview him about Formula One during our eight years working alongside each other, but he always said hello when I met him, and was never anything other than friendly.

I was, though, able to talk to him when he returned to racing with Toyota at the Le Mans 24 Hour Race in the late 1990s. Nothing is more gratifying for a journalist than when you enter a crowded press conference like there was at La Sarthe on the day before the event, see Brundle at the centre of attention on the top table, only for him to look across, acknowledge my presence and give me the thumbs up, which means, "I'll be coming over to talk to you as soon as I've finished with this lot." That was one occasion when I didn't need to stand behind him in order to attract his attention. His interview was better than Ozzie Osbourne's as well.

15

F***ing Brilliant ... the Perils of the Football League Play-Offs

There's a moment towards the end of any Play-Off Final, whether it's been at Wembley or before that in Cardiff's Millenium Stadium, when Greg Whelan from Sky TV looks at me and I look at him, and we sigh and prepare for battle. Few sporting situations are harder to work in than on the pitch after the final whistle goes. Time was, of course, that the media wasn't even allowed on the hallowed surface. That's all changed now, since we pay the money and we want the access. It's improved our lot, but has also led to some extremely tricky on-air moments.

To put this into some sort of geographical and chronological context I'd better explain where Greg and I are when the final whistle blows. We watch the game from a couple of rows behind one of the dug-outs, just behind the substitutes. The angle is quite low and it's often not that easy to work out what's going on. I can never understand why managers prefer to watch from ground level, but that's by the by. On our side of the pitch, which is the opposite side from the TV cameras, the sun is always shining straight at you, and of course, after six months of sitting freezing in press boxes up and down the country, because the sun is always behind you (once again for the benefit of the cameras) play-off weekend is always the hottest of the year. You look for just one tiny cloud to give you respite, but it never comes and you're left to squint at the TV monitors to try and work out what's happened on the replays. You're also wearing a suit and a tie, because you never know which government minister or senior member of the Football League may be presented for you to interview.

So there we are, Greg and I, waiting for the final whistle. Just before the end we'll pop down to the tunnel to have a chat with the Sky floor manager Mick Howard. He'll then tell me which players TV are going to interview, so I know which ones I can go and speak with. Normally they'll take the manager and the scorer of the winning goal, but that still leaves you plenty to go at. I then tell the pitch reporter from the winning BBC local radio station so that he knows which people are out of bounds until after we've had them, so to speak. The reporter from the losing side has the toughest job of all, which is to go and glean reaction from the side which has just seen a seasons work evaporate in the space of 90 minutes. We also have to speak to them to maintain balance, but it's just about the hardest interview you'll ever do, and as Dave Jones, the former manager of Cardiff City, quite honestly admitted to me after they'd been defeated by Blackpool, "I don't really want to be doing this." Point taken.

So the final whistle blows and the contrast is as severe as you can imagine. At one end of the stadium players sink to their knees as supporters dissolve into tears. At the other end mayhem ensues. Team members hug each other and dance around, and behind the goal 30,000 fans go bananas. The public address system cranks up the volume as the announcer decides to play whatever cheesy tune best represents the moment (it's inevitably Status Quo) and in the middle of this Greg and I sally forth.

It's actually easier for him because he has the redoubtable Mick Howard with him, and Mick, being the doyenne of floor managers, makes things work. They also have a camera crew with them, so it's pretty obvious what they're about, and footballers always want to appear on the telly. On the other hand I have just my radio microphone and a set of headphones clamped round my ears as the producer says, "Right, just shout when you have someone to talk to, we're all listening."

So off I go into the maelstrom, first of all trying to find

someone who's played in the game, since the pitch is now awash with backroom staff, substitutes and any number of hangers on. Then you have to see if you actually recognise anyone who fits that bill, since these are teams you often haven't seen before.

In 2007, when the Play-Offs returned to Wembley for the first time in seven years, I was booked to work the whole weekend. The first match was the League Two Play-Off Final between Bristol Rovers and Shrewsbury Town, neither of whom were on my patch. The only person I recognised when I arrived before the match was Lennie Lawrence, Rovers' director of football, who I'd interviewed many times, first when he was manager of Charlton Athletic, then when he moved up to the North-East and enjoyed success at Middlesbrough. On the side of the pitch I made a bee-line for Lennie and he obliged with a thoughtful contribution, before introducing me to Rovers' young manager Paul Trollope. On the Shrewsbury side, manager Gary Peters wasn't talking, but fortunately his assistant was John McMahon, brother of former England international Steve, and the husband of Nicky, who I knew because she worked in the media department at Everton. So John represented Shrewsbury pre-match and all was well with the world.

Bristol Rovers won the game and I didn't think the studio would be that keen on post-match interviews, mainly because it was only League Two and they probably had other sports to cover since it was a Saturday afternoon. But the producer had other ideas and I was duly dispatched onto the pitch with the usual instructions, to interview anyone I could find. TV had already taken Paul Trollope and Richard Walker, who'd scored two of the goals, so that left me with ten players, none of whom I knew, and with Bristol Rovers wearing their famous blue and white quartered shirts, even that wasn't easy because the numbers on their shirts are difficult to make out at the best of times, let alone on the Wembley pitch.

Then I had an idea, which was to find Steve Phillips. Steve was the Bristol Rovers goalkeeper, so he'd be the only one wearing a goalkeeper's jersey. I also knew that he was a local boy, and that he'd previously spent ten seasons at Bristol City. When I found him, amidst the scarves and the hats and the general shouting, when he finally could hear me above the Status Quo music, we probably conducted a couple of minutes of pretty ordinary radio interview. The questions would have been along the "How do you feel?" line, and I doubt Steve will ever remember it. By the time we'd finished, TV had done with Paul Trollope, and Lennie Lawrence was around as well, so I gave the programme what they wanted, and we lived to fight another day.

The next day saw Blackpool beat Yeovil 2-0 as Simon Grayson laid the foundations for their eventual rise into the Premier League under Ian Holloway. This was a much easier afternoon, since I'd been to Blackpool a couple of times during the season, and I'd interviewed Simon. In other words, he knew who I was. Blackpool also had a splendid captain called Mike Jackson, who was experienced enough to be taking in the moment rather than dancing about like an idiot, and our departments links with the great Jimmy Armfield meant that we had a closer connection with the club.

Since that day in May 2007 I've been to Bloomfield Road many times and always enjoyed it. I've usually found Blackpool to be a welcoming club, mainly down to the efforts of Matt Williams, who doubles up as secretary and press officer, and who, as I write this, is now half the size he used to be. Three years later he was on the pitch again, as Blackpool celebrated their promotion to the Premier League in one of the best Play-Off Finals ever, when they beat Cardiff City 3-2. We'll come back to that, because between Blackpool's two marvellous days at Wembley came the afternoon that Hull City beat Bristol City, and Ian Ashbee provided me with my most unforgettable play-off moment, and believe me, I've tried to forget it many times!

Hull City had finished the 2007-08 season in style. They'd won eight of their last twelve regular season games to come third in the Championship table, behind West Bromwich

Albion and Stoke City. In the semi-finals they'd demolished Watford 6-1 over two legs, and were now faced with the big money match against Bristol City. Phil Brown, who'd taken over from Phil Parkinson in January, had achieved a remarkable transformation, carrying on the good work started by Peter Taylor.

Hull's renaissance is one of my favourite stories over the 20 plus years I've spent patrolling the football grounds of the north of England. In the late 1990s they very nearly went out of the league completely, as Mark Hateley tried to revive them and failed. Before that there were stories of disgruntled fans putting fish heads through the chairman's letterbox, and I only seemed to travel across to the ramshackle Boothferry Park to report crises.

I remember speaking to their manager Terry Dolan back in the early 1990s about a young striker they'd signed from North Ferriby United. I interviewed him and was intrigued by the way the player ended most of his sentences with the phrase, "D'ya know." That was a particular linguistic trait of those from the Hull area, and it made an interesting feature back in 1993. Little did I know that fifteen years later that same player would be about to write his name indelibly into the Hull City record books. If he wasn't already a legend, on that afternoon in May 2008, Dean Windass, for it was he, would score the goal which took Hull City into football's top flight for the first time in their 104 year history.

By then, of course, Hull had benefitted from the building of the KC Stadium, which housed both themselves and Hull FC Rugby League team. They'd also enjoyed four seasons under the stewardship of Peter Taylor, a fine coach who lifted the expectations of the Humberside footballing fans.

So the "Tiger Nation," a phrase coined by the then chairman Paul Duffen, descended on Wembley, hardly daring to dream that they could reach the promised land. They approached the match as if it were any other, arriving in tracksuits and staying in the dressing rooms until it was time for their warm up exercises. Bristol City wore the suits with the red roses in, they wandered onto the pitch and waved to their families, and by the time they came to play they'd probably expended far too much energy.

Phil Brown had actually taken expert advice and had kept his team out of the limelight until the hour before kick-off. He'd been to see Sir Alex Ferguson at Manchester United, and Fergie's advice had been straightforward. Phil told me that Fergie had said to treat this as just another game. So the players were told that they'd be able to speak with their family and friends on the morning of the game, but once the team met for their pre-match meeting and meal that would be that.

Those of us hoping for Hull interviews we were to be disappointed. Neither Brown nor his players emerged until after the team sheets had been handed in, and even then they went straight onto the pitch for their warm up. What Brown had done was to allow Brian Horton, his experienced deputy, to stand on the touchline, presumably observing Bristol City expending their energy with the pre-match Wembley rituals. Brian, known by everyone in football as Nobby, was quite happy to talk. Like Ferguson, he was another of that elite group of managers with over 1,000 games to his credit, and was someone I knew well from his days in charge at such diverse locations as Luton Town and Manchester City.

Whilst we may have cursed Phil for not being available pre-match, his tactics worked. In the 38th minute, Dean Windass volleyed Hull City into a 1-0 lead, which they hung onto until the end of the game. Hull had top flight football for the first time ever.

Down on the touchline as Mick Howard, Greg Whelan and I waited for the final whistle to blow, Mick issued his instructions. Sky TV would take Phil Brown and Dean Windass, and after that we could have who we wanted. As I'd been to Hull City's pre-Wembley press day I knew that one player who'd be good to talk to was their captain, a likeable Brummie called Ian Ashbee. Amidst the chaos I went looking for him, and duly found him, somewhere towards the Hull end of the pitch, sweating and smiling and taking in the amazing scene as a sea of black and amber danced in front of him.

The interview was, of course, live. Ian Ashbee neither knew nor cared that this was the case since he'd just become a Premier League footballer and was enjoying the greatest moment of his playing career. The term "journeyman professional" could have been made for Ashbee. He was an England Youth International who'd been moved on by his first club, Derby County, after making just one senior appearance. He'd spent six seasons at Cambridge United, before moving to Hull when they were a mid-table side in football's fourth tier. He'd come through the divisions with them, coming back after an injury which threatened not just his footballing career, but his ability to even walk again. Plenty of context then as he was approached by this microphone wielding reporter on the Wembley pitch.

Now my one rule about interviewing anyone at this exact moment is not to ask the question, "How do you feel?" although it's the one thing you're tempted to say. There is always a different way of asking the obvious, although with all the madness going on around you it's not easy to maintain your own high standards. This proved to be a case in point.

I'd done the hard work, and I'd found my interviewee. I'd told the producer to come across, and Ashbee knew he was about to be spoken to.

PRESENTER: "So let's go down onto the pitch and join Peter Slater."

ME: "Thank you, and with me is the Hull City captain Ian Ashbee. Ian, you're now a Premier League footballer. After all you've been through with Hull City, what does this moment mean to you."

ASHBEE: "It's f***ing brilliant."

ME: "Well, we are live down here, and everyone's pretty excited."

The interview did continue, although I never quite knew whether Ashbee was aware of the faux pas he'd just committed. I went on to speak to Phil Brown, Paul Duffen, and eventually, back in the tunnel, Dean Windass, who gave me a much more thoughtful interview than he'd done fifteen years earlier at Boothferry Park whilst clutching his Man of the Match Trophy. That live interview was recorded and sent around the country so that BBC local radio stations could re-broadcast it in their sports programmes. Strangely enough, the Ian Ashbee interview went the same way, without being edited. I don't know how many BBC stations found out how the Hull City captain had been feeling at that exact moment, but a BBC memo went out warning producers to check things more thoroughly in future.

A couple of years later, with the black and amber replaced by tangerine, I found myself back on the pitch speaking to Blackpool's players after they'd beaten Cardiff City to reach the Premier League, where, ironically, they'd replace Hull City. This time, as I spoke to Ian Holloway, Keith Southern, Brett Ormerod and the rest, I was able to say to them in the few seconds before we went on air, "Remember chaps, this is live, so no swearing please." It's my Ian Ashbee early warning sign, and, fortunately, the moment hasn't been repeated. But I suppose there's always a next time.

16

Bill Shankly is Surprised

Back in my early local radio days, it was a very rare event to be sent to cover a game away from home. Now it's quite normal for a station to have a dedicated commentary team to cover their club. In fact some BBC stations have more than one set of commentators, Radio Newcastle, for example, use Mick Lowes and John Anderson to report on Newcastle United, whilst Nick Barnes and Gary Bennett cover Sunderland. The same applies in Manchester where they go one better, using specific reporters for each one of their teams: United and City, Bolton and Wigan.

Like I said, in the North-East in the late 1970s we had neither the budget nor the technology to allow this. ISDN has meant that stations share costs, commentary lines are instantly available and you have exclusive access to the lines for the entire afternoon. In my early days the only way to broadcast was on the telephone and you had to hire these priceless instruments from whichever freelance or agency happened to be supplying them. And you often had to share the phone with other radio and newspaper journalists who were covering the same game.

This led to friction as radio stations began to proliferate and sports editors realised that sending your own reporter to the game meant that you had someone the listeners could identify with. It also meant that listeners received a better, more informed service. In fact one of the reasons I moved to Suffolk in the early 1980s was because the job meant that I was the dedicated Ipswich Town reporter, covering every game, wherever and whenever they played.

In Newcastle in the late 1970s though we didn't yet enjoy this luxury and instead had to rely on freelance reporters who were employed by the agency which owned the phones, or indeed the owners of the phones themselves. Sometimes they weren't very good, sometimes they were drunk, sometimes they thought they were reporting for newspapers and dictated copy rather than describing events for radio. It wasn't an altogether satisfactory state of affairs.

So when Newcastle United found themselves playing an FA Cup fourth round replay at The Racecourse Ground in Wrexham on February 6th 1978, I was thrilled to be told that I'd be travelling to North Wales to cover the game. We'd hired a phone from the local agency, although I'd be sharing it with a reporter from Radio City in Liverpool, a young man by the name of Clive Tyldsley, who's gone on to enjoy a fruitful career as a TV commentator for both the BBC and ITV.

On the same evening at The Victoria Ground in Stoke, one of our non-league sides, Blyth Spartans, were taking on Stoke City in a game which had already been postponed once because of the February weather. It promised to be a night of exciting FA Cup football. Wrexham were top of Division Three, Newcastle all but bottom of Division One. The sides had drawn 2-2 at St. James' Park ten days earlier, but the bad weather had delayed the replay until now. As for Blyth, no-one really gave them a chance of overcoming Stoke, despite the fact that Stoke were struggling in the bottom half of Division Two.

Because it was a night match, Metro Radio had agreed that I could also stay in a hotel after the game, and travel back to Tyneside on the Tuesday morning. I'd booked a room at a small establishment in a place called Redbrook Maelor, not far from Wrexham, and I arrived in plenty of time to have something to eat and head off for the game. The press box was cramped, Clive and I shared the phone, and the evening developed into one of those remarkable FA Cup nights which we sadly no longer see. Two giant killings took place on that Monday night and it proved a bitter sweet occasion for followers of North-East football.

At the Racecourse Ground Wrexham played Newcastle United off the park, beating them 4-1 with two goals from Dixie McNeill and one each from Bobby Shinton and Les Cartwright. Meanwhile in The Potteries, Blyth Spartans pulled off one of the most famous victories in modern FA Cup history, beating Stoke 3-2.

After the match I conducted a brief interview with the Newcastle manager Bill McGarry, but the players were, quite naturally, not keen to speak. However, events in Stoke now meant that Wrexham would be playing Blyth in the fifth round and I needed to find someone from the Welsh camp to talk about this remarkable turn of events. Looking around the dressing room area I spotted the former Liverpool manager Bill Shankly.

Shankly had left Liverpool some four years earlier and was now acting as a football consultant for the Wrexham manager, Arfon Griffiths. I walked across and nervously asked if he could spare me a few moments to talk about the game. He agreed and I started my tape recorder. I knew that he wouldn't suffer fools so I tried to keep the questions simple and straightforward, about the game and about Wrexham's hopes for the rest of the season. My final question was about Blyth Spartans and their famous win at Stoke that night.

ME: "Bill, what are your thoughts about what's happened this evening. Wrexham have beaten Newcastle whilst Blyth Spartans have won 3-2 at Stoke. Are you surprised?

SHANKS: "Son, the only thing that surprises me is that people are surprised."

It was a great ending to the interview and meant that when Wrexham played Blyth in 12 days time my radio station would have this priceless interview with a football legend.

So off I went, back to my hotel, hoping that the bar would still be open and that I could enjoy a late drink with the hard work done.

As I walked into the hotel, the lights were on and clustered around the bar were a group of five or six men, who looked like they'd been there for some time. I approached and asked the barman for a drink and one of the group asked me where I'd been until this time of night. I explained that I'd just returned from Wrexham where I'd been watching the game. They were football fans and so they started asking me about the score and the nights other news, including the Blyth Spartans result.

"What's that over your shoulder?" one of them enquired. I explained that it was my tape recorder, and after further questioning told them that I had an interview with Bill Shankly on the machine.

Well that lit the blue touch paper because this group who were, it turned out, agricultural feed sales representatives, came from the Liverpool area, and wanted to hear the great man speak. I rewound the tape and played it. They particularly liked the final answer, when Shankly said that "the only thing that surprises me is that people are surprised." They liked it so much in fact that when it came time for me to buy a round they refused to accept my offer. Instead the cry came up to "Play us another Shankly." So I did and enjoyed a convivial evening with a group of complete strangers and a tape recorded interview.

The following morning I remember waking up with a rather splendid hangover and dim recollections of the night before. At the foot of my bed was my tape machine and on the machine was the cause of my dry throat and throbbing head. I switched on and pressed play and there was Shankly, still surprised and still an excellent few minutes of radio, which my sports editor was delighted to receive when I eventually arrived back later that day.

As with so many of these experiences, I sometimes wonder if there's a group of ageing sales reps, who still meet in the bar of that pub and talk about the night they shared several rounds of drinks with a tape recording of the man who built the modern Liverpool Football Club..

17

North-East Enders (the Newcastle United Soap Opera)

Newcastle United came into my life long before I ever started reporting on them, and there have been many times since that I wished they hadn't.

My family moved to Tyneside in the summer of 1967, after my dad had been promoted to the Inland Revenue Valuation Office at Kenton Bar, to the north of the city. I settled into the fourth form at Gosforth Grammar School and for a while kept my footballing loyalties with the team I'd left behind on Teesside, Middlesbrough. The problem was, because none of my family was in the slightest bit interested in football, I couldn't actually go and see the 'Boro play.

Believe me I tried, but with only my pocket money the train fare alone was prohibitive, and so I started to go and watch the local team instead. Later on, having acquired a Saturday job this meant I was limited to midweek matches, but Newcastle United had qualified for Europe and so I ended up witnessing their march to the Fairs Cup Final of 1968-69, enjoying such epic encounters as the semi-final victory over Glasgow Rangers, when half of Scotland seemed to have occupied the Gallowgate End.

Whilst at Sheffield University, United went on an FA Cup run, reaching the final in 1974. During that run they beat West Bromwich 3-0 at The Hawthorns in just about the best game I've ever seen, where "Jinky" Jimmy Smith became indelibly marked out as my footballing hero.

After university, when I came back home, St. James' Park

became a more regular haunt, usually standing in the Centre Paddock with Les Manderson, one of my Gosforth neighbours, occasionally venturing further afield, to Bolton or Derby to watch away games. But by the summer of 1976, instead of standing on the terraces watching Micky Burns and Alan Gowling, I was standing in the dressing room at the Benwell training ground, being introduced to my heroes as the young man who'd be coming amongst them with a microphone as Metro Radio's new sports reporter.

The first game I ever reported on was at St. James' Park on August 28th 1976. Newcastle United played Bristol City. Both sides had played two league games, and both had collected a win and a draw. The game finished 0-0 and I had to broadcast a three minute report at the end of it. What luxury, except that very little had happened.

Match reporting gradually became part of my routine, but more usually, especially once Metro introduced a Friday night sports programme, I drove down to Benwell on a Friday morning to collect a couple of interviews. These were often with the manager Gordon Lee and one of the players. In those days you just waited in the car park or by the changing rooms until your chosen player arrived and then they'd stand and speak to you for a couple of minutes.

That Newcastle side had some excellent talkers in it. Geoff Nulty, Burns and Gowling were university educated, Irving Nattrass and Alan Kennedy were young and bright, Tommy Cassidy and Tommy Craig were always obliging, it was a great introduction to the business. Of course, it couldn't last, because Newcastle's board of directors hated and distrusted the media, and would do anything in their power to make life difficult for us.

When builders moved in to construct a new indoor training facility the press were banned for a time, because the club's hierarchy accused us of stealing the bricks. When Richard Dinnis replaced Gordon Lee as manager, the directors appointed him on the same evening that Liverpool were winning the European Cup for the first time. Instead of watching the game, like every other football fan should have been, we were hanging around in the car park at the ground waiting to speak to the new manager.

This was the same car park where the BBC's Stuart Prebble once produced a memorable piece of television, as the new chairman of the club, Bob Rutherford, on the day of his appointment, refused to speak to waiting journalists and headed off down the slope to his car. Prebble told his cameramen to pan round and track Rutherford as he walked, later dubbing on the soundtrack: "And so, with no message for the fans, the man with the future of this great club in his hands, turned on his heels and left." It was a damning indictment and did little to heal a climate of distrust, which existed at the club until John Hall and Kevin Keegan started the revolution in 1992. Stuart later went on to form the company which brought *Grumpy Old Men* to our TV Screens, and having stood alongside him for hours in that wretched car park I think I know where some of his ideas for the series came from.

Anyway between Gordon Lee and Kevin Keegan, Newcastle United had seven managers, and I've interviewed them all many times. Since Keegan left in 1997 another ten have tried, including Keegan himself for a second attempt. The club deserves its own chapter because of its constant ability to shoot itself in the foot, so we'll start with Richard Dinnis.

Richard Dinnis (1977)

Dick Dinnis was Gordon Lee's assistant when the pair moved from Blackburn Rovers to replace Joe Harvey at Newcastle United in 1975. He'd been a school teacher before turning to football coaching full-time, and for a young reporter he proved to be a thoroughly decent chap, which was never the right sort of characteristic to be manager at St. James' Park.

Up at the Benwell training ground, as I waited for either Gordon Lee or one of the senior players to be interviewed, Dinnis was always happy to pass the time of day, enjoying his role in a team which was doing well in the league, and which had recently reached a Wembley final for only the second time in 20 years. The players both liked and respected him and it was a good place to be. Then Gordon Lee left and went to Everton, in the middle of the season. Dinnis was appointed caretaker manager and steered the team to fifth place in the First Division, which was enough to qualify for the UEFA Cup the following season. It could have been even better, but the team lost four of their last five games.

Despite the club finishing in its highest position in the league for 25 years it didn't seem that Dinnis had done enough to convince the board of directors that he should be given the job on a permanent basis. As the season ended he was still only in temporary charge. The players wanted him to take over, the fans seemed to be behind him, but the men in power continued to stall. Then, as I've mentioned earlier in this chapter, they offered him the job on the night Liverpool won the European Cup.

The following season started well, with Newcastle beating Leeds United 3-2 on the opening day at St. James' Park, but that was as good as it got for the new manager. Newcastle lost their next ten league games, were dumped out of the League Cup by Millwall and were demolished in the UEFA Cup by a Bastia side inspired by the Holland World Cup star Johnny Rep.

On Friday November 4th 1977 I made my usual morning journey to Benwell to interview Dinnis before the weekend game at home to Bristol City. I was totally unprepared for the interview Dinnis was about to give me. It was like listening to someone writing their resignation letter. He criticised the board for not being ambitious enough and for not giving him the money to strengthen his squad. At the end of it, I sat there and asked him if he was sure he wanted me to broadcast what he'd just said, because I knew that once the directors heard this he'd be in serious trouble. He told me that he knew exactly what he was doing and that I could put the whole lot on the air.

Back at Metro Radio's studios my sports editor listened to the interview, agreed that it was really hot stuff, but shared my reservations, since he also liked Richard Dinnis. But a story is a story, the interview led the sports bulletins, and the following Wednesday Dinnis was sacked.

He later went on to manage in the North America Soccer League, and I remember conducting a transatlantic phone interview with him whilst he was there. He came back to England in the late 1970s and went back to teaching, running soccer camps in the USA and doing some co-commentating for BBC Radio Lancashire.

Many years later our paths would cross again as I covered Blackburn Rovers in both the Premier League and in Europe. We once spent a couple of days together on a trip to Finland, where, in a small town called Kouvola we watched the locals trying to enter the *Guinness Book of Records* by singing karaoke non-stop in a tent in a local car park. They were halfway through it when we arrived, in the middle of a Finnish heat-wave in July 2008, and continued until they broke the world record after more than 445 hours. Richard Dinnis and I had come a long way from Benwell to Kouvola, but as we enjoyed the Scandinavian summer the conversation occasionally drifted back to Newcastle in the 1970s, and that fateful interview. Dick had no regrets about saying what he said. He wanted out and used me as the vehicle with which to do it. The only sad thing was that he was replaced by someone with whom I found it hard to develop as close a relationship. That man was Bill McGarry.

Bill McGarry (1977-1980)

After the rather cosy times I'd enjoyed with Richard Dinnis, the arrival of Bill McGarry came as something of a shock. Whereas Dinnis was chatty and amenable, McGarry was one of the old school, something of a martinet with the players and not very forthcoming in interviews.

It all started well enough, when I secured the first radio interview with him at BBC Television's studios in New Bridge Street in Newcastle. It was a Saturday and Bill had just arrived in town to watch his new club play Arsenal. He'd agreed to do a TV interview "down the line" with Bob Wilson, and I was able to grab a few minutes with him as he waited in some ante-room. He was perfectly pleasant and agreed to come out to our studios on the Monday night to do a phone-in with the fans. This was common practice in those days, and no manager ever refused.

United lost the Arsenal game 2-1, in front of a dismal crowd of just 22,880 and the biggest cheers were reserved for Malcolm MacDonald as he took his seat in the stands. He was the Supermac the supporters wanted, not the Supermac the board had just appointed as manager. McGarry won his next three games, but it was to be a false dawn. On Boxing Day 1977 Newcastle lost 4-0 to Manchester City at Maine Road. It was a game I'll never forget for all the wrong reasons.

I'd been told I could go to Manchester to cover the match and duly set off in the Metro Radio news car. At Hartshead Moor services on the M62 the car expired with a blown cylinder head gasket. I managed to hitch a ride in the back of a van and arrived at the ground five minutes before kick-off, with my preview written under trying circumstances amidst a group of Newcastle fans travelling to the game, who all knew how to write it better than I did.

Denis Tueart scored a hat-trick for City, Colin Bell came on as a substitute and a young full-back called Martin Gorry made his first, and as it later proved, his last Newcastle United appearance. By half past five on Boxing Day evening my work was done but I was stuck in Manchester without a lift home. Happily one of the Newcastle players, Irving Nattrass, learned of my plight, and I was offered a ride in the back of his father-in-laws Jaguar, which was quite a way to finish quite a day.

As I said, those three wins were a false dawn and apart from a 2-0 victory at Leeds on January 2nd, Newcastle United didn't win a single league game for the rest of the season. The team which had achieved that fantastic finish twelve months before now came in second from bottom, eleven points from safety in the days when it was still two points for a win. Not only were they relegated, but McGarry's side also suffered that resounding defeat to Wrexham in the FA Cup, an evening which is detailed elsewhere in this book.

By now I'd been forced to develop a different way of handling the new manager. There was no informal gathering up at the training ground with him. I had to speak to him down at the ground when he'd finished up at Benwell. At first some of the national newspaper journalists forced me to conduct my interviews in front of them, so that they were able to hear everything we talked about. Then they'd tell me to go away, so that they could talk to McGarry away from my prying ears. It's a common enough way of doing things, after all the newspapers don't want their "exclusive" appearing on the local radio station before they even go to print. I grew to understand and respect this, but what I didn't like was the rudeness of some of the north-east press mafia, who treated me with disdain, as if what I was doing didn't matter. One day, acting more courageously than I felt, I had it out with the press, in front of McGarry. I pointed out to both parties that whilst I understood that they had a job to do, I did as well.

We agreed that I'd speak to the manager on my own, away from the newspapers, and that's exactly what happened from then on. McGarry once banned me from the ground after his goalkeeper Steve Hardwick told me he'd asked for a transfer. The story was true, but that didn't seem to matter. Then there was the occasion when rumour had it that McGarry was going to take over at Stoke City, his home town club. The press arrived at St. James' to speak to the manager, convinced that he was going to tell us he was on his way.

In the foyer of the club, McGarry addressed the assembled group, giving us the news that, yes indeed Stoke had approached him to take over, and ... wait for it ... he'd turned them down and decided to stay. My heart sank, as did the collective hearts of the rest of us in the room. We were stuck with him.

After hovering around the lower part of mid-table, Newcastle won their last three games that season and finished eighth, but no-one was fooled into believing that the corner had been turned. The following season they finished ninth, but that was even more disappointing in a way because on

January 9th 1980 they were top of the table. They won just one of their last 16 games, with their leading scorer Alan Shoulder, who signed after helping Blyth Spartans to the quarter-finals of the FA Cup the previous season.

Although Bill McGarry and I understood each other by now, it was obvious to me that my career, which by now was entering its fifth year at Metro Radio, was unlikely to bring me the glories of European football, cup finals and, well, success as long as this man was in charge. By the third week of August 1980, Newcastle had lost two of their opening three league games, and had only just beaten Bury in the first leg of a League Cup tie. On August 29th McGarry was sacked and replaced by Joe Harvey on a temporary basis as the club looked for a new manager.

That night's edition of the *Newcastle Evening Chronicle* shows Joe in the St. James' Park car park, at the centre of attention again. Just behind him you can spot a man with a tape recorder and a microphone. I don't know if it's possible to detect the smile on my face, but inwardly I'm happy. On the way home that night I stopped off to buy a bottle of champagne, to celebrate the departure of a man I couldn't get on with. I hoped that Newcastle might look to bring Bobby Robson from Ipswich to take over, but instead they appointed Arthur Cox, who if anything, was harder to talk to than McGarry. Within three months I'd left Tyneside for good, pitching my tent in Suffolk alongside Bobby Robson.

It was to be another three years before Arthur Cox guided Newcastle back into the top flight of English football. That side contained Peter Beardsley, Chris Waddle and someone who was to become part of a Tyneside revolution nearly a decade later. His name was Kevin Keegan and his managerial style was as far removed from Bill McGarry as it was possible to be.

As for McGarry, I only saw him once more. I was walking down The Strand in London, on my way to the annual Football Writers Dinner when I came upon him walking in the same direction. He was fit and tanned from his time working in Southern Africa, and his hair appeared to have turned orange, probably dyed for all I knew. He greeted me like a long lost friend and seemed a bit confused about the function he was going to, since I don't think he'd been before.

I took him under my wing and guided him into the Savoy Hotel where the dinner was taking place. By then I was the BBC's football producer, well known by the football fraternity, and Bill McGarry was a former England International who had enjoyed a reasonable managerial career at Wolves and abroad and who was delighted to have been invited. We arrived as equals.

It was a strange turn-around from those dark days on Tyneside when he'd been a difficult interviewee and when he'd banned me from the ground. As we parted I didn't dare tell him that I'd once bought a bottle of champagne to celebrate his sacking. It just didn't seem right.

Arthur Cox (1980-84)

Arthur Cox had the most ferocious handshake of anyone I've ever met. He'd grip yours firmly and just hold on for as long as was proper, so that you knew exactly who had the upper hand, both literally and metaphorically. He arrived at St. James' Park from Chesterfield in the autumn of 1980, a much younger man than Bill McGarry, but not a media dream. For example, if you phoned Arthur in his office, he'd start his replies with a sort of low pitched growl which sounded much like the dialling tone and made you believe he'd actually rung off. Maybe it was a ruse designed to make unwanted callers do just that.

By the time Arthur arrived I was already making other plans. I'd applied for a job on Radio Orwell in Ipswich, with the chance to report on Ipswich Town, who were currently top of the First Division. The fact that Arthur had started to steady the ship mattered little as I'd travelled down to Suffolk for an interview and had been offered the job.

I continued to cover Newcastle games, indeed I remember going to Stamford Bridge where Chelsea won 6-0, but my mind wasn't on it, and by the time Kevin Keegan arrived as a player and United actually won promotion back to the big time, I'd been happily settled in Suffolk for over three years, and hadn't been back to Newcastle once.

Jack Charlton (1984-85)

The next time I reported on a match at St. James' Park was in the 1984-85 season, when Ipswich were overwhelmed 3-0 by the side of Waddle and Beardsley. Jack Charlton was manager then, a brief interlude which ended when he resigned after a pre-season friendly. I never interviewed Big Jack when he was in charge of Newcastle but he later reappeared in my journalistic life, first as the manager of The Republic of Ireland during the 1988 Euros and then the 1990 World Cup, and eventually as one of my more eccentric summarisers.

When I was a producer I could usually rely on Jack if I needed an expert for a game at St. James'. He only lived a dozen or so miles outside of the city in the village of Dalton near Ponteland. Ok so he'd often be late and seemed in a world of his own, but once the microphone was opened he was very good value. Probably my favourite moment was when he arrived on New Years Day having resolved to give up smoking. He'd come armed with dozens of small chocolate coated sweets, I think they were called Dime Bars, and proceeded to chain chew them throughout the game.

Incidentally I should also mention here that I used two other members of Jacks family as summarisers from time to time. The first was his brother Bobby "Our Kid", who often helped me out on Manchester United's early European trips after the Heysel ban was lifted. He did let me down once, in Madrid, when his wife insisted that he sat next to her instead of with me. I had to search pretty hard to find a deputy, and was fortunate when Colin Addison, one time assistant to Ron Atkinson at Atletico Madrid, appeared at the directors box entrance. Colin filled in for me, and helped out again at Old Trafford when we needed a summariser after the commentary line went down at our main game. As far as Newcastle United was concerned of course, Addison was manager of Hereford in that never to be forgotten FA Cup tie.

The other "Charlton" who helped out was Jack's uncle Jackie. Jackie was a shy, retiring sort of chap, who needed an awful lot of persuading to even come and talk on the radio, but he did it for me. He was making a living as a Sunday newspaper journalist when I started on Metro, but he'd also tried and failed as a manager, taking charge of Ipswich Town before Bobby Robson arrived. The Cobbold family described him as "a lovely man," the Geordies just called him "Wor Jackie" because Jack Charlton's uncle was Jackie Milburn, whose statue greets you as you turn into Barrack Road to be confronted by St. James' Park.

Willie McFaul (1985-88)

Wille McFaul was the eternal caretaker manager who was eventually given the chance to do the job full-time.

As a player he'd been an immensely popular goalkeeper in almost a decade at the club. He finished in 1975, just before I started my reporting career, but like other Newcastle United stalwarts he'd stayed in the region, working on the coaching staff and was often given the job of bridging the gap between one manager and the next.

At the start of the 1985-86 season he was thrust into the limelight when Jack Charlton resigned following that pre-season friendly when he'd received abuse from the fans. I was a long way away from this as I'd recently joined the BBC in London, but in November 1985 I found myself back on Tyneside, producing the main OB of the afternoon at St. James' Park between Newcastle United and Chelsea.

I'd left as a young reporter five years before, now I had access to all parts of the ground and a seat in the directors box. I felt extremely proud of how far I'd come in that short period of time as I sat directly above the paddock where I used to stand watching. Sadly Newcastle lost 3-1, and I realised that my job had changed when I found myself ushering the Chelsea manager John Hollins, who I'd got to know quite well, into our BBC interview room to take part in *Sports Report*. Those national newspaper journalists who'd tried to shut me out when Bill

McGarry arrived weren't allowed into such a hallowed place, and I certainly wasn't going to help those who'd made my life difficult. I made an exception for Tony Hardisty of the *Sunday Express*, who'd shown me great kindness when I was younger, and who now had an exclusive opportunity to speak with Hollins after he'd conducted his live interview for us.

That one incident taught me that if you help others, one day they'll remember and help you, and I hope it's a principle I've managed to stick to throughout my career. I've always tried not to make enemies, but sometimes in this business there are those who can make enemies when there's no dispute to be had. Some of them use their positions of "power," to make life difficult for people, like the journalist who used to run the press box at Old Trafford. I shan't name him and anyway he's no longer with us, but if he could upset my outside broadcast then he would do, and if I organised seats for foreign broadcasters once Manchester United returned to Europe, then there was hell to pay.

Most broadcasters and journalists rub along together pretty well. If someone's ISDN line goes down and there's a spare circuit, then it's lent out. If a microphone breaks or someone forgets a set of headphones, then another pair will usually be found from somewhere. At the top of the food chain there may rancour and disagreement, but amongst the foot soldiers we all help each other.

Willie McFaul lasted three years in the job. I didn't interview him much, but he was kind enough to appear on one of my football previews and he's still involved in the game, having spent time once as manager of Guam, which is somewhere in the Pacific. By the time he left I was on my way back to the north, as too was someone I'd helped along the way, and who was to help me, before becoming part of an event which showed me that the world of football media was changing. Before all that, though, I need to talk of West London taxi cabs, directors box seats at Oxford United, and being invited to lunch with Newcastle United the day before they failed to win promotion to the First Division. The man who links all these events, and who surveyed the North-East scene from a flat in Tynemouth was the one and only Bald Eagle.

Jim Smith (1988-91)

My favourite interview with Jim Smith, and there have been many, was just before the 1986 League Cup Final at Wembley. Smith was then manager of Queens Park Rangers, and as luck would have it, QPR had reached the final only to be playing Oxford United, the team Smith had left in order to take over in West London.

I'd known Jim briefly during his time at Oxford, before Robert Maxwell had taken the strange decision of not improving his contract. In fact I'd used him as a summariser for Oxford's semi-final home leg against Aston Villa, for the simple reason that he'd been offered just one ticket for the game and had wanted to take his wife with him as well. Because he was working for the BBC, he sat in the commentary box and she was able to have his ticket, so all was well.

A few weeks later, in West London, I'd been sent to interview Jim Smith prior to the final. There had been plenty of media interest of course, because of his links with QPR's opponents, and Jim was very busy with plenty of commitments both at Loftus Road and elsewhere.

By the time my turn came the manager was about to leave the ground to head across London for some other function. He was very apologetic, but I knew that this was my one and only chance to secure the piece that my editor had asked for. We'd helped Jim out and I hoped he might return the favour. So I tried my luck and asked him where he was going to. He told me he was heading along the West Way to Central London and that the taxi was waiting outside. I suggested that since Broadcasting House was on the way we could actually do the interview as he travelled. Jim seemed agreeable to this and so off we went, the two of us in the back of a black cab, heading out through the streets of Shepherds Bush and onto the flyover.

Fortunately the traffic was typically terrible and by the time we'd nosed our way down the Marylebone Road I'd been able to cover all the topics I needed to make a piece which was used right across the networks. Even better, whoever was paying for Jim to make the journey picked up the fare, so it cost the BBC nothing.

QPR lost the final 3-0 in a game which provided Oxford United with their finest hour. Jim Smith stayed at Rangers until the autumn of 1988, when he moved to replace Willie McFaul at St. James' Park. In January of 1989 I moved back north from London to take over as the BBC's senior producer in the north of England. Jim Smith and I were back in business again.

I remember telling him on one occasion that he was now in charge of "my team." That was probably when Manchester United knocked Newcastle out of the FA Cup on their way to securing Alex Ferguson's first trophy at Old Trafford, but my next real memory is of an act of kindness from Jim, perhaps returning the favour I'd done him four years earlier when I'd allowed him to bring his wife to that Oxford United game.

Whatever the reason, the occasion was the eve of the final match of the 1989-90 season. Newcastle were in with a chance of promotion back to the First Division, having been relegated the year before. That final match was at Middlesbrough, who were in need of the points themselves to avoid relegation.

I'd tracked Jim and the team down to a country house hotel on the outskirts of Teesside, and had conducted a number of interviews which I was going to send back from the local BBC radio station. Before I left though, Jim insisted that I join him and the team for lunch. So there I was, sat between the manager and Kevin Dillon on the day before their most important game of the season, I felt privileged indeed.

The following day, at Ayresome Park, Newcastle being Newcastle, lost 4-1 and missed out on automatic promotion. This meant they had to take part in the play-offs against their hated local rivals Sunderland. They managed to lose that one too, and so were resigned to another year in the second tier of English football. Later the following season Jim Smith resigned, describing Newcastle United as "unmanageable."

His next job was at Portsmouth, where he took the side to an

FA Cup semi-final, and from there he went to Derby County, taking the club into the Premier League, at the same time as they moved to their new Pride Park Stadium. Jim revelled in being manager of a decent club with a decent ground and as always greeted me with a broad smile and a firm handshake.

One day I visited the Derby training ground, which in those days was next to a dual carriageway to the south of the city. I'd gone to record a feature about their Costa Rican striker Paolo Wanchope, who'd been making a name for himself in the top flight of English football. I interviewed Jim, who was his usual ebullient self, talked to the player, and then to the Derby first team coach, a young man I hadn't come across before. He talked well, even suggesting that Wanchope was "virtually uncoachable, because if he doesn't know what he's going to do next, how do we?"

I was very taken with the interview, and when the coach moved onto his next job, as assistant to Alex Ferguson at Manchester United, I followed his career with interest. Later on he would become a regular on the other side of my microphone when he took over as manager of Middlesbrough. His name, of course, was Steve McLaren, and I was to follow him one summer's day to the town of Enschede in Holland, when he was given a chance to resurrect his career after an unsuccessful spell as England manager. Later we'd meet occasionally in Europe, and he'd always stop for a chat, perhaps recalling simpler days at Derby or at Middlesbrough's Riverside Stadium. He'll appear again later in this chapter.

Kevin Keegan (1992-97)

I was driving home from playing squash with my friend Ken Ibbotson when the news came on the radio. "Ossies Dream is over," the announcer said, "And Kevin Keegan is the new manager of Newcastle United." I turned to Ken and said: "Well, that's a publicity stunt if ever I heard one." How wrong I was proved to be.

It's perhaps harsh to suggest that Kevin Keegan was a lucky manager, but there were several particular circumstances surrounding his tenure at St. James' Park, which gave him the best possible chance of success.

First of all, when he arrived things could hardly have been any worse. With only a handful of games to go, Newcastle United were in danger of being relegated to the third tier of English football. It was unthinkable and certainly had never happened before. Any improvement would reflect well on the new manager, in fact just avoiding the drop would help enhance his reputation.

Secondly, he arrived in the midst of a boardroom revolution. Once John Hall had taken control of the club, it had been his decision to dispense with Ardiles and appoint Keegan, who, let's not forget, had had no previous managerial or coaching experience. It seemed an appointment made with the heart rather than the head, but it worked. Newcastle survived the drop, and started the following season as if they owned Division Two. They won their first eleven games and went on to take the title by eight points and regain their place in the top flight, which was now the Premiership, where all the money was.

Hall gave Keegan the money to build a team capable of challenging for the title. With players like David Ginola and Andy Cole, then latterly the returning prodigal son Alan Shearer, Newcastle suddenly became a byword for exciting, attractive football. Hall rebuilt the stadium to its present majestic 50,000 plus capacity, and talked about building a club for "The Geordie Nation" rather along the model of Barcelona. The ground couldn't accommodate everyone who wanted to come and watch and the games were beamed live into local cinemas for those who weren't fortunate enough to have a ticket. All this came not long after crowds had dropped to a weekly average of around 15,000, which was unthinkable on football mad Tyneside.

I loved it all, and particularly I loved Kevin Keegan, who at the centre of it all never lost his enthusiasm for the game or his ability to provide interview gold whenever he was asked for it. I know he's most famous as a manager for his rant against Alex Ferguson during a live Sky TV interview after a game at Elland Road one night, but I'll remember him for the many times he answered all my questions thoughtfully and with an intelligence that showed him wanting to be part of the conversation which a radio interview should always be.

In fact, I'd go so far as to say that if I had to name the best interviewee I've ever come across, week in week out, Kevin Keegan would be top of the list. Former World Motor Racing Champion Jackie Stewart runs him pretty close, but for what he brought to Tyneside, I'd have to give the award to KK.

It would be hard to choose any specific interview which singled the man out. After all, not only did I have to speak with him on a regular basis when he was at Newcastle, our paths also crossed again when I returned to covering northern football after my stint on Formula One, and found Kevin in charge at Manchester City, where his round table chats on a Friday lunchtime at the Carrington training ground always yielded talking points.

I remember speaking to Newcastle striker Les Ferdinand when the players used to train at Durham University's Maiden Castle Sports Centre, and seeing Keegan approach mischievously from Ferdinand's blind side and silently taking the mickey as Sir Les talked to me. I remember waiting ages for him as he and Terry McDermott played endless games of head tennis in the gym, extending their unbeaten record against all-comers.

There's a photograph on my study wall taken from a *Sunday Times Magazine* article, which shows Keegan, headphones on, talking down the line to *Sports Report* as I stand next to him, listening to his pearls of wisdom. On another occasion, in the same place, I was about to interview him live for the same programme, and we were talking off-air about Phillipe Albert, the Belgian defender who'd been such a success during his time at St. James' Park. Kevin was making the point about how Albert sounded exactly like the actor who played the policeman in the comedy series *Allo, Allo*. "You should hear him," Kevin was telling me as we waited for our slot. Then, adopting a French accent he continued. He'll say "Zat referee, ee's a f***ing c***. Kevin wasn't wearing headphones, so he didn't know that we were still 30 seconds away from going live. After he'd uttered the expletives I said, pretending the programme had actually crossed to us, "Kevin Keegan there, joining us live here on national radio."

The look of shock on his face was priceless. He thought he'd been caught swearing live in front of two million football fans, and in the split second before I told him that the only other person who'd heard him was me, he must have thought he was in deep trouble. Fortunately he immediately saw the funny side, because that was the man he was.

I remember the day he resigned, as I put together a feature on Northumberland Street with a mournful trumpeter playing in the background, and the delight when Mike Ashley brought him back, sadly for only a few months. Unfortunately in some quarters Kevin Keegan is regarded as a quitter. They say he should have won the title in 1995. They say he shouldn't have signed Faustino Asprilla. They don't know him, and neither did I the day I said his appointment was nothing more than a publicity stunt. The only other manager who's been able to repeat Keegan's success on Tyneside is Bobby Robson, and his story is elsewhere in this book.

The man who took over from Keegan is someone else who has crossed my path on numerous occasions. I witnessed his home debut for Liverpool in 1978, when he also took over from Keegan. I interviewed him when he was in charge at Anfield, then at Blackburn Rovers when he won the title for Jack Walker. I've seen him be awkward and generous in equal measure. I also interviewed him after the match when he decided to quit his beloved Liverpool. The next man in the Geordie firing line was Kenny Dalglish.

Kenny Dalglish (1997-98)

Those who know Kenny Dalglish well say he's one of the most witty, engaging individuals in the game. Others see him as a right old curmudgeon, a smart arse who makes interviewing him a nightmare. Over the years I've known him I've seen both sides of his character. I did the last interview he gave as manager of Liverpool in 1991, up in the press room at Goodison Park following a 4-4 draw against Everton in the FA Cup. Two days later he'd resigned from the club he'd represented as player and manager for 14 years. I was with him at Anfield four years later when Blackburn delivered the Premiership title to Jack Walker. We spoke in the tunnel just minutes after Rovers had edged out Manchester United, and he couldn't have been more fluent and articulate, despite the fact that he was eating a cheese sandwich at the same time. Kenny was on form that day because his team had won, and that's probably at the bottom of the Dalglish conundrum. He's a winner to the extent that when he loses he's miserable, and when he wins it's almost as if he's proving a point to those who aren't like him. Chris Waddle was an unsuccessful manager because the players he was in charge of frustrated him so much. They couldn't pass a ball 60 yards and land it on a sixpence, and Chris reckoned the only ones who could understand his anguish were those who'd been able to do what he could do as a player. Dalglish was the best at what he did, and I think he distrusted, and still distrusts anyone who dares to question his motives, tactics or demeanour, and that includes all the media.

But there's another side to Kenny. First and foremost he's intensely loyal to Liverpool Football Club and anyone else who employs him, but particularly to Liverpool, and this is entirely understandable. We're talking about him in a Newcastle context of course, but the links are impossible to ignore. Dalglish made his home debut for Liverpool against Newcastle, wearing the number seven shirt made famous by Kevin Keegan. When he took over at St. James' as manager he was following the same man, but whilst he delivered more to Liverpool than Keegan ever did, he was to prove nowhere near as successful on Tyneside.

True, he took United to second in the table, to a Cup Final and to a Champions League victory over Barcelona but his signings weren't popular, and many of them were past their best. I thought that he'd mellowed as a person when he arrived in the North-East, and Graham Courtenay, who became his press officer for a while, won't have a bad word said against him. Graham also says what others who know Kenny well say, that when you switch off the microphones and cameras, and put away the dictaphones and notebooks, he's fantastic company. Dalglish lasted just 20 months on Tyneside.

Kenny Dalglish can also help the media. There's something you never thought you'd read, but I know, because I saw it happen. It was the Friday before the Sunday when Blackburn took the title, and it happened at the Rovers training complex at Brock Hall, up in the Ribble Valley.

The media interest that day was intense, and so Blackburn had scheduled a certain amount of time before training for the interviews to take place. The media were allowed down to the bottom complex at the club, which meant passing through security. But if you weren't there for the press conference, then there was no way you'd be allowed down. This is now common practice at all major football clubs.

Charlie Lambert, who was then BBC *Look North's* sports reporter, had a real problem. I think it concerned his cameraman, and I believe he'd had to go to the doctors or the dentists and he wasn't able to go to the conference at the right time. This meant that although Charlie was there, he couldn't do any filming on one of the biggest days of the year for his programme.

Now Charlie and Kenny went back a few years, back to their days on Merseyside, and Charlie went to explain his dilemma to the manager. He could do the interview, but only later in the day when his cameraman was available. Kenny understood the situation perfectly. He said to Charlie, "Come back after training and I'll speak to you. I'll make sure security know, because if you go back to your office without anything you'll be in serious trouble". So *Look North* got their interview, Charlie escaped the telling off of all time, and Kenny proved he was human after all.

Ruud Gullit (1998-99)

Ruud Gullit also took Newcastle United to an FA Cup Final. Like Dalglish he was one of the world's best footballers. I know, I was in the Olympic Stadium in Munich when he and Marco van Basten won the European Championship for Holland.

To be honest, I didn't interview him very often. All I do remember is that he was much taller than I expected and that he was extremely arrogant, as maybe he had a right to be given what he'd achieved in the game. However, he made one serious mistake, a mistake so bad that it lost him his job. He left Alan Shearer out of the Newcastle side for a derby game against Sunderland. He'd also fallen out with another of Keegan's stars, Rob Lee, refusing to give him a squad number.

Three days after the Sunderland game I was in the paddock at Spa ahead of the Belgian Grand Prix. I was chatting to the former Radio One DJ David "Kid" Jensen when my phone rang. It was one of my colleagues telling me that Ruud Gullit had resigned. Good riddance, and a shame, because he was the best in the world at one stage. Perhaps he should never have come to Tyneside.

Bobby Robson (1999-2004)

I've written much about Sir Bobby in other parts of this book, so I shan't add to that here. My only surprise was that he never came to Tyneside earlier than he did. If ever manager and job were meant to be it was Bobby and his beloved Newcastle. Fans will remember that the team won 8-0 in his first home game, It was a sad day when Freddie Shepherd decided to dispense with his services. In terms of Newcastle United's development what followed made Robson's tenure seem even more successful.

Sadly for me, he was sacked just as I was leaving Formula One to become the north of England football reporter. I'd still been able to conduct plenty of interviews with Bob when he came back to the North East, but I'd have liked to spend more time in his company. As it was, Newcastle managed to outdo even themselves when naming Robson's successor.

Graeme Souness (2004-06)

I was at Ewood Park in Blackburn, I think it was some sort of sponsorship event, when the news came through that their manager, Graeme Souness, had emerged as the man to take over from Bobby Robson. The mood was one of shock, not because Rovers wanted Souness to move, but because, so rumour had it, he was on the brink of being sacked by them anyway.

Let me say here and now that I admired Graeme as a player, and that as an interviewee he was always honest and straightforward, never ducking an answer. It's just, well, he should never have been given the job at St. James' Park. He spent far too much money on players who, quite obviously, weren't worth it, the worst being Jean-Alain Boumsong, the most expensive being Michael Owen, and biggest failure being a name which still makes United fans shake with a mixture of either terror or hysterical laughter, a Spanish striker called Albert Luque. Newcastle only saw the worst of the first, Owen was always injured, and Luque played like a rabbit startled in the headlights every time he received the ball. Souness also had a habit of falling out with players, Craig Bellamy, no shrinking violet himself, being the most obvious casualty as he left for Blackburn, who by then were starting to flourish under the canny stewardship of Mark Hughes.

Graeme was a disciplinarian, not easy when you're surrounded by millionaire prima donnas. However, I admired his stance on April 2nd 2005, one of those days when your game is meandering to a close then suddenly you become the centre of the sporting universe for a while.

Newcastle were playing Aston Villa, and losing, when I saw in front of me something which I'd never seen before. Two Newcastle players, Lee Bowyer and Keiron Dyer, were fighting, and they were fighting each other. Referee Barry Knight quickly moved in and sent them both off. My studio had pictures of all the Premiership games and when I buzzed in and told them to concentrate on mine, they started seeing what I was seeing on my monitor. The long and the short of it was that no-one could quite work out what had triggered this.

The talk back between London and Newcastle then went into overdrive. After the match I'd laid my equipment out, ready to interview anyone who might be able to talk. Souness had other ideas though. He confronted the situation like a man and came straight into the press conference, along with the two players, who were made to apologise for their behaviour, sitting in front of the media like a pair of naughty schoolboys. But that was that, all sorted, done and dusted in the space of a few minutes. I respected him for that.

I also admired him on a February night at the City Of Manchester Stadium, when he must have realised the game was up. Newcastle lost, the away fans unfurled a banner saying "Souness Out," but Graeme being Graeme he came out to speak to me, vowing to fight on as manager. He was fired the next day. It was his last managerial job, but the dugouts loss is the TV studios game, as he's carried his no nonsense approach into punditry. I said it many times when he was there, and I'll say it again. I liked Graeme Souness enormously, I just wished he'd never been manager of my club.

Glenn Roeder (2006-07)

Glenn Roeder had more going for him than Souness ever did. For a start he understood Tyneside, having played almost 200 times for the club in the 1980s. He was also their academy director, and when Souness left, Roeder took over as caretaker manager. He turned the club's fortunes around, and as an interviewee I always found him to be approachable and courteous, although maybe a little more guarded than his predecessor.

As results improved, the clamour for Roeder's appointment on a permanent basis grew. One Saturday afternoon at St. James', I asked Alan Oliver, who covered United for the *Newcastle Evening Chronicle*, if it was worth having a bet on Roeder becoming the next manager. Ollie told me he was a shoe-in for the job, although there was a dispute with the FA over Roeder not holding a UEFA Pro-licence. Undeterred by this I went home, after another Newcastle victory, and went onto the betting exchange "Betfair" where I discovered, to my amazement, that Roeder was 36 – 1 to be the new manager. I immediately put £30 on him, and two months later collected the biggest win ever in my rather limited gambling career.

So I'm grateful to Glenn for that, and also for his enthusiasm for the Inter-Toto Cup, a competition much derided by some, but loved by those of us who enjoy being in Slovakia or Estonia in July watching football instead of waiting for the other stuff to begin. Newcastle actually won the competition, but it wasn't enough to keep Glenn in his job. What followed was a dark period in Newcastle's black and white history, and it resulted in another time in my life where I've actually wanted them to lose matches in order to have a manager sacked.

Sam Allardyce (2007-08)

As with Graeme Souness, I really like Sam Allardyce and we get on well, but I bet he wishes he'd never accepted Newcastle owner Mike Ashley's offer of becoming Newcastle United manager after Glenn Roeder was shown the door.

I've never interviewed Ashley, but then neither has anyone else. He's famously reclusive and also extremely rich through his company Sports Direct. He's had a kind of love hate relationship with the fans, but they hardly hated him more than during Allardyce's brief but unhappy tenure at St. James'.

I first knew "Big Sam," as a player at Sunderland. He was a no-nonsense central defender, certainly not the sort of person who one would expect to go on and become one of modern footballs most forward thinking managers. I first interviewed him as a manager when he was at Blackpool, although the story that night was more about Chris Kamara and Bradford City, who overcame a 2-0 home deficit to win 3-0 at the tumbledown Bloomfield Road and reach the Play-Off Final. I remember putting Kamara on the line to talk to Trevor Brooking, who was presenting the show that night. Needless to say Kammy was hardly backward in coming forward, and has hardly stopped coming forward since.

Allardyce was quickly sacked by the Blackpool Chairman Owen Oyston, who was in prison at the time. It proved to be a poor decision.

I next interviewed Sam when he was riding high in Division Three with Notts County, and I remember the most difficult job was condensing his interview into a three to four minute piece for radio. Sam could talk about football forever, and often did.

After Notts he went to Bolton, where we'd often sit round a table at The Reebok, me, Sam, Jack Dearden from BBC Manchester and the other radio reporters as he held court. So successful was he with Bolton that he was linked with the England job and we had to ask him about it. Sam is an imposing presence and I vividly recall Jack saying to him: "Don't hit me Sam, but I've got to ask you about the England job." There's then a silence, after which Jack can be heard saying, "You're going to hit me, aren't you?" He didn't of course, he just gave him that Sam Allardyce grin and then said ... nothing.

So what went wrong on Tyneside? Well first of all Panorama broadcast a programme accusing, in a rather unconvincing way, Sam's son of unscrupulous dealings in his work as a football agent, implicating his father along the way. Sam immediately "did a Fergie" and refused to do any more interviews for the BBC. When he left Bolton shortly afterwards and shipped up on Tyneside, imagine how I felt. Here I was, the BBC's north of England reporter, and I couldn't interview two of my highest profile managers.

To make matters worse, Newcastle started Sam's first season in charge extremely badly, playing some dreadful football in the process. It all came to a head on Boxing Day 2007, when United lost 1-0 at Wigan. Mike Ashley was at the game and he, like me, couldn't help but hear the constant chanting, to the tune of the Pet Shop Boys *Go West*, "We're shit, and we're sick of it."

Match of the Day compounded the situation by focusing on two fans shouting angrily at Allardyce, telling him in no uncertain terms that he didn't know what he was doing. He surely couldn't last much longer. Even Mike Ashley would have to bite the bullet. I have no idea what Sam was thinking through all this, because he didn't speak to the BBC, which only made me want his reign to end even more.

I was actually in TV Centre in London when Ashley sacked Allardyce and I did a lap of triumph around the sports room before joining Peter Allen in the 5 live studio to say why I thought Big Sam had lost his job. I mentioned that one of my colleagues had opined that Sam never really understood what managing Newcastle United was all about, that he never bought into the culture of the club. That was a lie, since the person who'd said that was me.

After he left St. James' Sam went to Blackburn, where he was disgracefully sacked by the Venky Family. As I write this he's at West Ham, and the last time I saw him he gave me one of his bone crunching hand-shakes before joining me live on air to talk about another win. It's a funny feeling to know that here is someone who can be so media friendly and who brings the best out of teams who wouldn't normally do as well as they do, and yet at one stage, especially on that Boxing Day in Wigan, all I wanted was for him to be as far away from my team as possible.

Kevin Keegan (2008)

Mike Ashley now needed to pull off a PR masterstroke if he was to win over the Newcastle fans, and to be fair to him he managed it. In February 2008, with United playing an FA Cup replay against Stoke City, a small figure, dressed in black, reappeared in the ground. Kevin Keegan was back in charge, and all was right with the world.

Suddenly St. James' Park and the training ground at Darsley Park in the east end of the city were happier places to be. One of the best interviewees I'd ever known was back in harness, and the programmes loved it. So did I, except that most of the time interviews had to be conducted in an echoing changing room, which wasn't the best place.

The 2008-09 season started with hopes high on Tyneside, and Keegan's Newcastle duly responded with a couple of decent results. But behind the scenes all wasn't well. Mike Ashley had employed Denis Wise as one of his backroom team, recruiting players without Keegan's say so. There were certain members of staff no-one had heard off, no-one knew exactly what they were doing.

I recall my last interview with KK, ahead of the game against Arsenal at the end of August 2008. It took place in the indoor sports hall at Darsley Park, a vast improvement on the echoing changing room we were normally forced into. At the time I was sporting some three day stubble, which I thought to be quite fetching. As the interview ended his final words to me were "you need a shave by the way." Saying that he turned and walked across the indoor pitch and, shortly afterwards, walked away from the job for the second time.

What followed this time was jaw dropping even by the standards of this most remarkable of football clubs.

Joe Kinnear (2008-09)

Why Mike Ashley ever thought that Joe Kinnear could manage Newcastle United is beyond my comprehension. Joe was a jovial sort of guy, and I'd interviewed him enough times, first when he was at Wimbledon, then latterly at Nottingham Forest. But he had a history of heart problems and he certainly didn't endear himself to the North-East press corps by swearing at them during his first press conference, and vowing to sort them out.

He never did and under his stewardship the club, which John Hall and Kevin Keegan had lifted out of the gutter, now found themselves relegated to The Championship. The so called "Cockney Mafia" employed by Mr Ashley didn't hang around, neither did Joe Kinnear.

Alan Shearer (2009)

Alan Shearer, or "God," as he's affectionately known in our house, was only Newcastle's manager for a few games at the end of the 2008-09 season. He couldn't save them from the drop, and realised, I think, that the pundits couch was a much safer place to be than the dugout. But he was Newcastle's manager, and this is where he appears in the book. However, Alan Shearer and I go back much, much further than that, further than a few chats in that echoing changing room at Darsley Park as he tried to lift the spirits of a club which had been brought to its knees by another spell of appalling mismanagement.

Like the Knopfler Brothers, Alan Shearer is a graduate of my own Alma Mater, Gosforth High School. I used to live on the Regent Farm Estate and he used to live on Park Avenue, a road I'd often walk down, either on my way home from school, or going down to The Three Mile Inn on the Great North Road. He lived on one side of the railway track and I lived on the other.

We've spoken on countless occasions and he knows the connection, not that he'd ever go around saying, "Hey, you know that lad from the BBC, he used to go to my school." Well I don't think he would! I'll single out just a couple of significant meetings, starting with a phone call one morning from the office telling me that there were unconfirmed reports that Kevin Keegan had just broken the British transfer record to bring Alan Shearer to St. James' Park.

Now this was in the days before rolling news and sport, so I had time on my side as I headed up to Blackburn's training ground at Brockhall to see if anyone would say anything. I did have to stop once to do a live interview for *The Jimmy Young show*, my first and last. Of course we weren't allowed past the security guards, and the gaggle (nowadays it would be an armada) of press were kept out on the road.

After a while a Jaguar car approached up the hill from the training complex. It was Alan Shearer and to be fair to him he stopped and wound the window down. He did this because Alan had always been a courteous and amenable chap, always one of the Blackburn players ready to come and speak. On this occasion though, all Alan would say was that he couldn't say anything. Having said this he drove off. Mind you his silence said it all.

You could understand his dilemma of course, Newcastle

United were on tour in the Far East, and Keegan and Hall wanted to make the most of this transfer, a deal which had been financed partly by Scottish And Newcastle Breweries, who were the clubs sponsors. A few days later, in the full glare of publicity and in front of thousands of adoring Geordies, Shearer was paraded at the ground. He'd come home, and had come home for good.

After that he'd occasionally be selected for interview, first at Maiden Castle, then when the club moved their Training HQ to Chester-le-Street, and finally to Darsley Park. Alan was always affable, although possibly not the sort of person to give you a back page lead.

I would like to mention one moment with him, which highlights the pressure of that hour between five and six o'clock on a Saturday afternoon. Shearer had just returned after a long injury, and had, if memory serves, come on as a late substitute in a home game at St. James'. We reporters had recently been issued with new digital recording machines, Mini-Disc Players they were called, and it meant that you could cue up an interview by its track number, rather than in the days of tape, where you had to find the right place on your machine by trial and error.

I'd managed to grab the first post-match interview with Shearer, and I had it on my mini-disc player. I had the confidence to tell the studio to just cue it in from London and I'd play it out. They don't always like doing this, but here was the first Alan Shearer interview after his comeback, and they wanted it now. So I plugged up my ISDN, connected the mini-disc, pressed play to make sure I'd recorded the interview, and then pressed pause so that we were ready to go.

As I've already mentioned, these were new machines, and what I didn't know was that after a short period of time the pause button simply switched itself off and you were left with nothing. That's exactly what happened as Ian Payne was cueing in my Shearer interview. What was I to do? I just pressed play again and hoped. After a short pause the machine came back to life, the interview played out, and the producer came back on the line congratulating me for a fine piece of journalism. If only they'd known?

So Alan Shearer, from the temporary dressing rooms as Ewood Park was being re-built, through the European trips under Dalglish and then Ray Harford, back to Tyneside and all those magical moments in a black and white shirt, thank you. If I thought I'd lived the dream, then he certainly had, not bad for a couple of kids from Gosforth.

Chris Hughton (2009-10)

Shearer couldn't save Newcastle, but the man who did restore pride to the club was a quietly spoken Londoner, who'd played many times for the Republic of Ireland, and who just went about his business in a matter of fact way.

Chris Hughton always greets me like an old friend, with a firm handshake and an enquiry about my health. Like many people in the game, I'd just seen him around over the years both as a player and a coach and he and I were part of the scenery I suppose.

For a while he was just the caretaker manager, the man given the chance to pick up the pieces. In those days he'd always be asked if there was any news about him taking over permanently, and he'd always answer that he didn't know. In fact Chris was the ultimate professional interviewee, answering questions without telling you anything. But we forgave him because his team kept on winning, and when he was sacked we all said how much we'd miss him.

He went on to manage Birmingham City, then Norwich and latterly Brighton, where he's brought them success after decades in the football wilderness. He remains understated in a world of super-egos and always remembers those of us who have crossed his path in the past. People use the phrase "one of the nicest men in football" rather too much sometimes, but it's one which can be fairly applied to Chris.

Alan Pardew (2010-14)

Alan Pardew was an unpopular appointment for two reasons.

Firstly the Toon Army loved Chris Hughton, and secondly they saw Pardew as another of the "Cockney Mafia" and they'd had enough of them.

In the long run he proved them wrong and left under his own terms, despite several occasions when the fans would have happily driven him to the airport and put him on a plane back to London.

In terms of my contact with him, I'd say his interviews were right up there with Keegan and Robson: articulate, intelligent but very streetwise. Alan Pardew knew what was required when dealing with the media which is what top managers are now trained to do. It can't be easy in the Premier League of the second decade of the 21st century when you're needed to front up – even after a bad result – and do at least two TV interviews, a number of radio interviews and a press conference, all within an hour of the game finishing. I say required because it's a contractual obligation. The media organisations call the tune since they put the money in which oils the wheels.

Pardew even managed to develop a winning team, qualifying Newcastle United for Europe. But when results went wrong, he wasn't allowed the leeway of some of his predecessors. I've been at St. James' when there have been protests against him both outside and inside the ground, and it was perhaps no surprise when at the end of 2014, Pardew resigned from Newcastle to return to his spiritual home as manager of Crystal Palace. It seemed a marriage made to last, but it didn't, and at the time of writing Pardew is without a club. But when he left, of course, Newcastle United were a club without a manager.

John Carver (2014

There should be a section in the football managers' manual warning "number twos" about the perils of stepping up to become the main man. The game is littered with examples of those who've been successful working under great bosses, from Brian Kidd to Mike Phelan and beyond, but who never managed to make the transition upwards. John Carver appears to be one of those.

Another likeable Geordie whose love for the club was in no doubt, Carver had been Alan Pardew's right hand man, and when Pardew left, Carver took over. From his point of view it was an obvious choice to make. If you're a lifelong fan and someone offers you the chance to run the place, you're going to take it.

Carver grabbed the opportunity with both hands, making all the right noises in his media interviews. Unfortunately for him, as with many before, he couldn't motivate the team and they only avoided relegation on the final day of the season. Carver had to go.

Strangely, if anyone is a conundrum of someone who succeeded as a number two, then as a number one, and then failed, it was the man who was about to become the next occupant of the hottest of hot seats.

SteveMcClaren (2015-16)

It can be a peculiarity of my job that sometimes a whole season goes by without me being sent to cover a particular club. That happened in 2015-16 resulting in my missing Steve McLaren's unfortunate reign at St. James' Park completely. That isn't to say that I didn't know him; far from it. In fact I'd interviewed him many times over a long period starting when he was Jim Smith's assistant at Derby County, as detailed earlier in this chapter.

As I mentioned then, we'd crossed paths on Teesside, in the Netherlands, Nottingham and latterly in Derby where he'd been joined by another coach who features elsewhere in this book, the genial Cumbrian Paul Simpson. Simpson recently guided the England Under 20 team to victory in the World Cup incidentally.

Between them Steve and Simmo almost took Derby into the Premier League, only being denied by a late Bobby Zamora goal for Queens Park Rangers in the Championship Play-Off Final at Wembley. The following season they were favourites for promotion until the wheels came off, partly because of rumours linking McClaren with the job at St. James' Park. So it was no surprise when he was appointed in the summer of 2015. He knew the North-East, he was English and he had a track record which included some success. What could possibly go wrong?

What did go wrong was that McClaren couldn't win matches. Newcastle hovered near the foot of the table, the manager cut an increasingly desperate figure on the touchline and in March, only nine months after arriving, he was sacked.

In fact apart from sporadic successes at Middlesbrough and FC Twente, Steve McLaren's career has generally gone downhill. After Tyneside he went back to Derby and it didn't work out. For me his career is a conundrum. He's a brilliant coach, a fine interviewee and yet he can't quite seem to consistently show that undoubted ability as a manager. By the time you read this he may well have resurfaced somewhere else. I like Steve and I hope he succeeds again. As for the man who came riding over the horizon to replace him on Tyneside? He's someone from a completely different league, regarded as one of the best coaches in the world and, once again, someone I'd had the privilege of meeting before.

Rafa Benitez (2016-)

For a time when I was the BBC's North of England football reporter, my Friday routine was quite simple. I'd drive over to Merseyside, first to Everton's Finch Farm training complex, then across to Liverpool's headquarters at Melwood. At both places the radio reporters would gather in a small room to conduct a pooled interview with the two managers. Everton's supremo was David Moyes, who must wish he'd never left them, at Liverpool it was Rafa Benitez, a man whose legendary status in the Anfield Pantheon was assured when he guided the team to European Cup glory in 2005.

I immediately liked Rafa. When we were huddled in that room, away from the cameras, he was courteous and very funny. He was amused that I'd started taking Spanish lessons and insisted on trying to correct my rudimentary grasp of the language. Off the record he'd tell you quite a lot; on the record – unless he had an agenda – he was far more circumspect.

When he left Anfield he became something of a managerial nomad with spells in Italy punctuated by a brief period in charge of Real Madrid; that is if anyone can ever say they're in charge at The Bernabeu. He even rocked up at Chelsea and I caught up with him one winter night in Prague, where, eyes sparkling mischievously, he wondered if my Spanish had improved.

So when he was handed the almost impossible job of keeping Newcastle United in the Premier League, Tyneside held its breath. If anyone could, Rafa could. In the end he couldn't and it seemed like he wouldn't stay to try and take the club back up to the promised land. For once though, Mike Ashley managed to do something to please the Toon Army. Rafa stayed and guided United back at the first attempt.

So it came to pass that the next time I met him was in the radio room at St. James' Park. I asked him about his family, who were still living on The Wirral, and he told me he was having difficulty understanding his daughter, who'd developed a Scouse accent. We joked about how hard it must be for him to understand the Geordies and, as always, there was that twinkle in his eye, Rafa enjoying himself.

Just like Pardew, Allardyce and many others of the modern game, Rafa understands the demands of the media and manages to play them along superbly. I dread to think what Bill McGarry or Arthur Cox would have made of it all. Recalling these managers has also taken me on a journey through the way the business has changed over the years. But some things haven't altered mind, Newcastle United remains one of the biggest soap operas in English football; A club ready to shoot itself in the foot at any moment. I hope I'm around a little longer to document it all.

18

A Weekend at Gleneagles with Mark Knopfler, Captain Mark Phillips and Jackie Stewart

The BBC used to broadcast a programme on Saturday mornings called *Sport on Four*. It was aired between nine and nine thirty on Radio Four, and was presented by, amongst others, Tony Lewis and the late Cliff Morgan. It also had one of those catchy signature tunes, written and performed by Van McCoy. If you were a feature maker, it gave you the opportunity to produce material which wouldn't see the light of day on radio sports' other output, and some of my happiest memories have been working for "SO4" as it was called on the rota.

I once went to Wilmslow to talk to Peter van der Zyl, a Cheshire based Sri Lankan whose one ambition was to represent his country in the luge at the Winter Olympics. Peter had made a practice run in his front driveway, which involved a start ramp coming down from his garden shed and a modified skateboard. Peter told me that he knew he'd made a good start when he hit the hedge on the far side of the road outside his house. Fortunately for Peter, and for his neighbours, he lived in a cul-de-sac, but even then he'd developed an early warning system so they knew if he was training. After all, no-one wanted Sri Lanka's great luge hope run over by a careless commuter.

Peter was a great interviewee, as was his wife Wendy, who spoke to me before heading off for her evening class in Welsh, and it made a terrific five minutes of radio for a Saturday morning.

My feature on the town of Oldham made headlines in the local paper, I went with Bryon Butler one day to interview Richard Branson in the drawing room of his palatial house in Holland Park, and on the one occasion when I actually produced the show I spent several anxious minutes on the telephone to the comedian Roy Hudd, as he leaned out of his front door waiting for the radio car to arrive.

But one memory stands out above all the others, and it's a demonstration of how one thing can, quite definitely, lead to another. It also reduced me to banging the floor of a rented house in Manchester, frustrated beyond measure.

It all started with Peter Churchill and Princess Anne's first husband, Captain Mark Phillips. When I joined the BBC, in the few short weeks before I was made football producer, I was given a portfolio of sports to look after. Amongst these was equestrian events. This meant organising our coverage of three indoor show jumping competitions: the Royal International, the Horse of the Year and the Christmas meeting at Olympia. It also meant a couple of visits each summer to Hickstead in Sussex,as well as some three day events, like the Badminton Horse Trials and the one at Gatcombe Park, organised by the aforementioned Captain Phillips.

Once I'd been offered the football job, I was relieved of all my other duties, but because my wife was a big fan, I asked to keep the equestrian job, so that she could come along with me and enjoy watching one of her favourite sports.

It was the golden age of show jumping, with characters like Harvey Smith and Ted Edgar competing for Britain against the mighty Germans and their exceptional horseman Paul Shockemohle. Peter Churchill was my commentator, he was someone the jumping fraternity knew well, and because of his contacts we were able to call upon riders like Graham Fletcher and David Broome to be our expert summarisers.

When it came to eventing Mark Phillips became a good friend of BBC Radio. He wanted us to be there to cover his weekend of action at Gatcombe and we were happy to oblige. Riders like Ian Stark and Virginia Leng quickly became regular contributors as Churchill and Slater developed the output.

Then in the spring of 1988 Peter rang me in my office in Manchester, where I was on the five month attachment which would eventually lead me to becoming the department's senior producer in the north of England. He told me that Captain Phillips was opening a new training centre up at the Gleneagles Hotel in Scotland, and he'd offered to give us an exclusive guided tour of the new facility.

I called Peter Griffiths, who was producing *Sport on Four*, and pitched the idea of Peter Churchill and I making a feature for the show about this new enterprise. It had everything a Radio Four audience could want, royalty, a luxury hotel, horses and an Olympic gold medallist. Peter Griffiths agreed to take the piece, and so a couple of weeks later I drove up to Scotland, met Peter Churchill at Gleneagles railway station, and set off for the hotel.

This was on a Friday afternoon and we'd arranged to meet Mark the following morning to be shown around the training complex, do the interviews and then head for home. I'd then take the tapes back to Manchester to edit them for the following weeks show. It meant that the rest of the evening was free, so we booked a table in the restaurant and retired to our rooms to get ready.

I'd noticed on our way from the car park to hotel reception that there were some pretty smart vehicles parked outside. One even had the memorable number plate JYS 1, and I wondered which particularly heavy roller was driving this. I was soon to find out.

I'd just checked into my room when the telephone rang. On the other end was Gordon Turnbull, who was one of our senior editors. He told me that it was Enzo Ferrari's 80th birthday the following week and that he'd like me to put together a feature about it. Since I was in a hotel bedroom in Scotland about to make a piece on show jumping I wondered how I might be able to do that.

Gordon went on to tell me that Gleneagles was playing host that very weekend to a clay pigeon shooting competition, which still didn't explain the link to Italy's greatest motor racing figure. He then revealed that the event was being organised on behalf of the Motor Racing Mechanics Benevolent Fund, to help raise money for those once involved in the sport who'd fallen on hard times. Gordon said that Jackie Stewart was in charge (JYS of course) and that there might just be one or two motor sport personalities who'd be happy to speak to me about the great man.

So much for a relaxing evening, I now needed to move into top gear in order to nail as many interviews as possible. It also occurred to me that there might be a third strand to this Gleneagles visit, as *Sport on Four* may well be keen on taking a piece about racing drivers shooting clays in the Scottish Highlands. So instead of one piece, with any luck we'd come back with three, and that would almost have paid for the bottle of wine which Peter and I saw on the menu, priced £167.10. We especially liked the fact that they'd added that extra 10p. We chose a bottle of the house red instead!

Now I'd done a bit of motor racing in my early days at the BBC. I'd worked at the British Grand Prix at Silverstone, so when I spotted the BBC Radio's motor racing man Simon Taylor in the bar, I knew that things were looking up. I explained to him about the feature on Ferrari's 80th and how I may also be able to make a second piece about the clay pigeon shooting weekend. Simon said he'd introduce me to Jackie Stewart and that he was sure everything would be fine.

I needed to find other voices of course, and as Simon and I spoke I started to notice possible contributors. Murray Walker was there, and Murray is always happy to talk about the sport he loves. Stirling Moss came in, and he could speak about his relationship with the great man. Former World Champion Alan Jones was nearby, and one of Ferrari's current drivers, Michele Alboreto had also turned up. This was like being a kid in a sweet shop, as one by one I approached these great talkers, and one by one they agreed to add their tributes.

Then there was JYS himself, Jackie Stewart, who I would get to know much better during my eight seasons covering

Formula One almost a decade later. He agreed to meet me the following morning, sparing me half an hour of his valuable time on such a busy weekend. It was remarkably generous, but then Sir Jackie is a remarkable man, as I was to discover frequently later in my career.

Gradually the piece began to take shape as Murray Walker, Simon Taylor, Stirling Moss and Alan Jones gave me their thoughts. Michele Alboreto told me to meet him before breakfast the following morning, which meant an early start, but since this was such a coup I didn't mind.

My excitement was also heightened by the presence of a rock superstar in the building. I was a fan of his music, but my reasons for wanting to meet him went much deeper than that.

Back in the early 1970s, when I was attending Gosforth Grammar School in the suburbs of Newcastle upon Tyne, one of my friends in the sixth form was a lad called Dave. Dave was a very talented musician and we'd often play boogie woogie piano together on the school stage during the lunch hour. He was much better than me. We were in the drama group and appeared in the school play together, we even sat on the same dinner table where we compared our experiences with our current girlfriends. We shared a similar taste in music and I remember breaking the news to him that Jimi Hendrix had died, as we sat together upstairs on a number four bus heading for the People's Theatre in Jesmond.

Once school was over, like so many we went our separate ways, to universities and colleges up and down the country, returning north less and less as the years went by. Then in 1977, as I was starting my career on Metro Radio, Dave reappeared on Tyneside, and came with a group of us to see a Martin Scorsese film at the Odeon Cinema. After the film I offered Dave a lift back to Gosforth in my Triumph 1300 car, and he accepted, along with another school friend, Malcolm Herdman, who'd just started working in the Record Library at Metro, and my girlfriend Alison, who by then was living with me in a flat not far from my old school.

Dave was in good form, talking about how he and his elder

brother Mark, who'd also been to Gosforth Grammar, had put a band together and how they were beginning to make progress. Malcolm and I took this with a pinch of salt, since Dave had always wanted to be a rock star, and playing a gig at London's Rock Garden didn't seem like the best way of conquering America. Our doubts were vindicated when he told us the name of the band.

"We're calling ourselves Dire Straits," he said, as I turned left from New Bridge Street and up towards The Haymarket.

Eleven years later, with Dire Straits one of the biggest bands in the world, I found myself in the same building as Dave Knopfler's elder brother.

By now you would have thought I'd been there, seen it, done it and bought several tee-shirts. I wasn't likely to be phased by someone who'd gone to the same school, and whose brother used to be in my "A" level English set. However, sometimes it all goes wrong, and my brief meeting with the elder of the two boys who'd once lived in Briarfield Road didn't work out as I'd hoped.

When I did eventually track Mark Knopfler down, I made the mistake of saying to him: "Ah, you must be Dave's brother." It wasn't a good start, rather like the time I asked Noel Gallagher what he'd been doing at a production of Stephen Sondheim's *Sunday in the Park with George*, I'd been to, only to discover that it was Liam who'd been there and not him. Rock star siblings don't always get on, and the Knopfler's had had musical differences which led to Dave leaving the band after just two albums.

I recovered enough to explain who I was, about my Gosforth Grammar School connections and that I would really like him to contribute to my feature about Jackie Stewart's clay pigeon shooting weekend. Mark Knopfler stubbornly refused to take part. As things turned out, I don't really think he could have added much to the material I'd already gathered, and anyway he was there, amongst other things, to record a piece for ITV about fast cars, and they were paying him a lot of money for the privilege. That damned Jim Rosenthal was doing the interview. Little did we know then how much time we'd end up spending in each others company. But that was yet another decade down the line.

Jackie Stewart did appear however, and we ended up talking about Ferrari, about the clay pigeon shooting, and about the forthcoming Formula One season, which allowed him to give his views on who might win the title, and about some of the new driver pairings. It meant that now, if I played my cards right I had yet another piece to offer Gordon Turnbull.

In the middle of all this, of course, Peter Churchill and I went off to make the feature we'd been sent to do in the first place, and Captain Phillips duly showed us around, giving us an excellent interview which *Sport on Four* ran the following week.

On that same day, *Sports Report* was going to air my feature on Ferrari's 80th Birthday. I was living in a rented house in Manchester at the time and listened to the programme in the front room, eagerly anticipating hearing my work go out on air. On my return from Scotland I'd spent a lot of time distilling the various interviews down into a feature of around four to five minutes. Simon Taylor, Murray Walker, Jackie Stewart, Stirling Moss, Alan Jones and Michele Alboreto provided an impressive cast list. To say I was pleased with the final outcome was an understatement. It was good radio and I was certain Gordon Turnbull would be equally delighted. It was due on air, I'd been promised, sometime after half past five.

Sports Report came on the air at five o'clock. I wasn't working that Saturday, since the big game of the weekend, the Merseyside derby between Liverpool and Everton, was being played the following day and I was producing the outside broadcast. I listened to the classified football results and the match reports, to the live interviews with managers and players, and then waited, and waited, and waited.

With time running out, the programme ran an interview with one of the Everton players about the game against Liverpool. It wasn't a particularly memorable piece, and had been conducted by someone from the BBC local radio station on Merseyside. After that was finished, on came the racing results, and the show went off air. In that little front room I banged the floor with frustration. That specially commissioned piece, which I'd spent hours recording and days editing, which included some of British motorsports greatest names, had been dropped so we could hear the views of a footballer so ordinary that I can't now remember who he was or what he said.

However, there's one rule in radio which I've always followed, both as a producer and a reporter, and it's that the editor's decision, whether you agree with it or not, is final. If you want to do the job instead of the one you're being well paid to do, then have a go, if not, then just shut up. So I never did complain about the fact that my feature on Enzo Ferrari's 80th birthday never saw the light of day. I knew that it was good and I hoped that someone, somewhere, had listened to it and that the timings on that afternoon had meant that the programme simply didn't have enough room to run it.

There is, I'm delighted to say, a happier ending to all this. A couple of weeks later, *Sport on Four* ran my feature on Jackie Stewart's clay pigeon shooting weekend, with contributions from many of the people who'd spoken about Ferrari, but not, of course, Mark Knopfler. Then as an added bonus, the week before the new Formula One season began, the Saturday afternoon show promoted the fact that it had secured an exclusive interview with Jackie Stewart looking ahead to the campaign. It was so good that they ran it in two parts.

Several years later Gordon Turnbull rang me and offered me the job of BBC Radio's Formula One pit lane reporter, working alongside Simon Taylor. I'd like to think that he'd taken into consideration my earlier piece which never appeared on the radio. Perhaps he'd listened to it and remembered. Indeed, if someone had told me on that miserable Saturday evening of floor thumping that I'd be given in exchange, eight wonderful years travelling the world reporting on F1, then I'd have taken the offer there and then.

Still, it was a good piece, and it's a shame that it never appeared on the radio.

19

If We Put the Microphone Next to the Air Conditioner it Might Just Sound Like a Helicopter (Faking It on the Tour de France)

When I finished my eight year stint covering Formula One in the autumn of 2004, I threw myself into reporting northern football. It was the reason I'd come back, my rationale being that if I didn't take on the job of northern football reporter then someone else might, and I'd end up losing all the work that I did when I wasn't doing the motor racing.

Things panned out pretty well, with my colleague Juliette Ferrington and I travelling the highways and byways of the region doing interviews and covering matches. But then came the summer, that short period of time between the play-offs and the pre-season friendlies (normally about four or five weeks it seems) when footballers go to the beach, and reporters hide in their back gardens, pretending to care about Wimbledon but really just itching for the madness to start all over again.

I enjoyed the tennis and The Derby, I even went along to the odd day of Test cricket at Old Trafford or Headingley, sneaking up into the *Test Match Special* box to see if there was any left-over cake (there never was). However, there was one event which always captured my imagination during those long, occasionally sunny days of June and July. The Tour de France, once just an exotic, slightly mad three week bike race, had become an increasing part of the British sporting schedule, and it had me gripped, from the crazy bunch sprints of the first week, then up into the Alps and the Pyrenees where stick thin midget climbers would race up to the summit, fighting their way through crowds of drunken Dutchmen, flag waving Basques and Norwegians dressed in Viking helmets. The whole cavalcade would finish on the Champs Elysees with someone trying to break away unsuccessfully, then we'd switch off the TV and lo and behold the football season was about to begin again.

BBC Radio's cycling coverage had been provided for a number of years by the excellent Simon Brotherton, affectionately known by his friends and colleagues as "Burgers". He'd built up the coverage to the extent that his reports were now as much a part of the radio summer as The Open Golf Championship and The Derby.

Burgers lived a double life though because as well as covering cycling for BBC Radio, he also commentated on football for both radio and television. This meant that in the early part of the summer he would often be found at either The World Cup or the European Football Championship Finals. With F1 behind me and the summer my quiet time now, it occurred to me that he might just need someone to help him out during a hectic schedule, so in the autumn of 2005 I penned an email to the executive editor of BBC Radio Sport, Graeme Reid Davies, saying that if Simon was struggling to fulfil all his obligations, then I'd be happy to offer myself as a cycling deputy.

Several weeks later Graeme sent me back a two line reply. "Peter," he said, "can you do the first nine stages of this summer's Tour de France please?" I was ecstatic. I was actually going to report on one of my favourite sporting events. In 2006 it started in Strasbourg and went up into Luxembourg and Holland before heading out to Brittany. I was to travel with producer Cath Davies and Graham Jones, the former tour rider who acted as expert summariser and driver of our SUV. Simon would arrive on the first rest day in Bordeaux, where we'd switch seats, I'd return home, and he'd follow the race to Paris.

Now whilst I'd been an armchair cycling fan for years, the only time I'd ever covered an event was when the Tour of Britain, or Milk Race as it was then known, had come through my patch. Basically that meant a stage finish in South Shields when I was in Newcastle, and a Round the Town Criterium when I worked in Ipswich. Now I'd be faced with calling home a sprint finish on the second day of the race, in a suburb of Strasbourg. That year we didn't do live commentary on the final hour of each stage as we do now, that was an innovation brought in a couple of years later, but the finish had to be called, since both BBC 5 Live and World Service needed it for their bulletins and for their archive. It was a daunting prospect.

Cath and I flew down to France on the Wednesday night before the event started on the Saturday with the usual prologue time trial. Graham would drive the van down from London, and we'd all meet up in the hotel on Thursday, so we could begin the process of collecting accreditation and doing interviews with the few British riders who were taking part. Back in 2006 there weren't many of them, just David Millar, returning from a two year doping ban, and young Bradley Wiggins, riding his first tour for the Cofidis team after his success at the 2004 Athens Olympics.

Now I was used to big media centres after my experiences in Formula One, but the size of the hall for the Grand Depart made them all seem pretty small beer. There was the accreditation area, there were all the sponsors trying to gain publicity from their booths, there were food stalls and souvenir stands, and then a giant hall filled with journalists from around the world. Amongst these were the British press corps, those who made a living from covering cycling and a couple of national newspaper men who'd been sent to cover the event. In a few short years, with Wiggins and Cavendish, Team Sky and the rest, that press corps would swell as the British started to gain a real foothold in the Tour de France, but on that June Thursday it was mainly the cycling specialists.

Cath was a tour veteran and knew these people, and one by one she introduced me to them. All wanted to know why

159

Burgers wasn't there, but they welcomed me into their circle – even more so when we all went out for a beer that evening. Amongst them were three men who'd become good friends and allies over the coming years, and indeed over the coming days when I needed their help more than I could possibly have known. They were the Fotheringham brothers, William and Alasdair, and Steve Farrand.

William wrote for *The Guardian* as well as being an accomplished author and contributor to specialist cycling magazines. His younger brother was working for *The Independent*, but was also an expert on Spanish Cycling, the more so because he lived in Spain and spoke the language fluently. Farrand, or Farrandino as everyone knew him, came from Oldham but had lived for many years in Italy, writing for the specialist publications on the sport in that country.

Around the barroom table that night there was much discussion about a Spanish based investigation into systematic drug taking in sport. It was called Operacion Puerta and wasn't just centred on cycling, rather on a doctor called Emmanuel Fuentes, who, it was alleged, was linked with major figures across a number of sports.

Walking back to our hotel that Thursday night, Cath and I found ourselves passing the place where the tour organisers were staying. Sitting in a circle on an outside terrace, deep in discussion, I noticed amongst others Jean-Marie Leblanc, who was coming to the end of his tenure as race director, and Christian Prudhomme who was due to succeed him. I assumed they were making their last minute plans for the start of the race.

The following morning we were making our way across Strasbourg to the media centre when my phone rang. It was the office in London bringing me the news that Operacion Puerta had chosen that day to publish its findings. Cycling was well and truly implicated, and at the highest level. Amongst those named were the German Jan Ullrich and Italy's Ivan Basso, who were two of the favourites to win the tour. The immediate outcome, the desk was telling me, was that Ullrich, Basso and half the Astana-Wurth team had been thrown off the race. 5 Live wanted me broadcasting immediately, and every other BBC outlet, from the *World at One* to *News 24* needed my expert analysis of the situation.

The only problem was that apart from that discussion in the bar the previous night I didn't really know much about Operacion Puerta. This was partly my fault but also the fault of the investigators for announcing their findings on that morning. No wonder Leblanc and Prudhomme had been in such deep discussion the previous night. They probably knew what was coming.

Cath set me up in an annexe of the press room with a broadcasting box known as a Comrex, and started fielding calls from everyone who wanted to speak to me. I went looking for any of the friendly faces I'd met for the first time the previous evening.

Fortunately I found both William and Steve, sat them down and said – because it was the truth – that I needed their help and quickly. I wrote down as much as they knew about the fast moving events, went and re-wrote it for broadcast, came back and ran it past them to make sure I wasn't making a fool of myself, and sat down to speak to the world.

Such camaraderie doesn't exist in all sports. Football reporters can be decidedly terse when they know something which could stop you appearing an idiot, but the cycling lads were just great. They understood that I was a rookie and made sure that I had the bare bones of the story correct. After that it was up to me to embellish and turn it into decent radio and TV and I'm delighted to say that we got away with it.

After that the actual race coverage was pretty straightforward. I called the sprint into Strasbourg, which was won by Jimmy Casper, and called it correctly, with a little bit of help from Graham who wrote down the word "Jimmy" on a piece of paper, since I'd had a mental block and could only remember the Frenchman's surname. We journeyed up into Holland on a blisteringly hot day, where the stage was won by a German rider called Matthias Kessler who was later to

161

test positive for illegal substances. There were no British riders to trouble the commentators, although I remember Bradley Wiggins being part of a breakaway group one afternoon.

On my final Sunday, a wet and windy day in Lorient, we finished up our work then drove down deserted roads all the way to Bordeaux. The roads were deserted that Sunday because that was the day of the World Cup Final and in Paris France were playing Italy.

We arrived in our hotel just in time to watch extra time, to see Zinedine Zidane sent off for his infamous head butt on Marco Materazzi, and then watch Italy defeat the home nation in a penalty shoot-out.

I'd survived my first Tour de France experience, and knew that my next chance would be in two years time when Simon would be covering the Euros and the Olympics. I looked forward to the possibility immensely.

The following autumn I persuaded Graeme to let me cover the newly re-constituted Tour of Britain, which started in Scotland and finished in London with a race around the historic landmarks of the city. This was as a precursor to the 2007 Tour de France, which would begin in London and include a road stage down to Canterbury. It wasn't as big as Le Tour, of course it wasn't, but Britain was gradually starting to embrace the sport. Our track cyclists had already achieved great things in the Olympics, and Team GB's Performance director, Dave Brailsford, had some great ideas in the pipeline, one of which, incredible as it seemed at the time, was to develop a mainly British team to compete in the Tour de France.

Sadly for me 2007 was Simon Brotherton's year to cover the race. I watched the Spring Classics and the Giro d'Italia on Eurosport, conscious that this time round all I would be was a spectator. I saw the highlights of the prologue time trial in London, and watched that incredible Sunday as the race snaked it's way south from the capital, the roads jammed with spectators, every town and village out there to support the race. It was very emotional and I wished I'd been part of it.

I then went back to covering the usual pre-season round of

friendlies and press conferences. On the day of the prologue I'd been to see Liverpool play at Wrexham, and I was back at Anfield the following Friday, a typically wet English summer day, to speak to Ryan Babbel, the Dutch winger who'd just been signed by Rafa Benitez.

As I walked into the ground my phone rang. It was Graeme Reid Davies and I couldn't quite make out what he was saying. The coverage inside football stadia isn't always brilliant and I was running a little late. I thought I'd heard him say that he might want me to go and cover the Tour de France, but I wasn't exactly certain. An hour or so later, with the interviews completed and sent, I rang him back.

What had happened was that Simon was going to have to come home for family reasons. It would only be for a couple of days, Graeme assured me, but they'd booked me on a flight from Luton to Geneva on Sunday morning. Was that OK? Of course it was OK, it meant that I'd be part of the great event once more, although no-one wants to take over in circumstances like that, with a work colleague forced to come home.

By 2007 there was a new cycling producer, someone I didn't know, someone who'd answered the job advert from his place at BBC World TV. Phil Sheehan was a cycling fanatic and a very useful road racer in his own right. We became good friends over the next few years, but that Sunday morning we were due to meet for the first time at Geneva Airport, where Simon would leave the van and I'd replace him, before heading off to Tignes for the first mountain top finish of the year.

That was the plan, but it didn't work out that way. The flight I was due to travel out on developed mechanical trouble, and the passengers all had to transfer to another plane in order to make the journey. I had to call Phil to tell him the news. It meant that I wouldn't arrive in time to do the change over and that we wouldn't be able to go to the top of the mountain to report on the finish. Phil and Graham Jones couldn't go without me, because I was the broadcaster and the nature of the Tour de France meant that we'd be moving on that night to Grenoble as the race continued into the Alps.

The solution was simple, and the truth can now be told, since the BBC thought we were at the top of the mountain waiting for the riders to arrive from Le Grand Bornard. Where we actually were was in the Mercure Hotel in Grenoble, eating a lunchtime baguette and watching Stage 8 on the television. Our excuse was simple. We'd never have been able to make it up the mountain at that late stage, and since we were only doing updates and not live commentary it wouldn't really matter.

But we had to sound authentic otherwise the listeners would know that we weren't where we said we were. So we rigged up our mixing desk accordingly, with me sat facing the television and my microphone just far enough away so that it picked up the excitable French commentary from the TV without it being distinct. That meant it sounded like the public address system which always keeps the spectators informed at the finish of each stage.

Next we needed to find some sort of background effects, something which would make it seem that we were at the finish. Phil noticed that outside the room was an air conditioning unit, and that if we hung a microphone outside then it sounded not unlike a distant helicopter. This would do the trick perfectly, since a lot of the TV pictures are taken from the air, and helicopter noise would make my reports sound even more authentic.

So from the comfort of Room 112 we commentated on a stage win for the Danish climber Michael Rasmussen, who also took over the leader's Yellow Jersey. Fortunately we weren't asked to send over any post-race interviews and within half an hour of the stage finishing we'd de-rigged and were off into town for dinner. This was a real luxury since the normal procedure at the end of each stage is to file voice pieces and two ways as the press tribune is demolished around you. The next task is to race back to your SUV, which Graham has usually manoeuvred into a more favourable parking space, and then head out of town on the route marked out for the organisation and media.

If you're on top of a mountain this means you're part of the Grand Evacuation, which sounds dreadful but which is actually quite a spectacle. The roads are closed to the general public until the evacuation is complete. This means that you have to join the team cars, publicity caravan and other media in one long line at the top of the peak. At a given signal, which means that the last rider has crossed the line and the stage is clear, we all begin to head off the mountain. You just slot into the line and go for it, driving at speed past the thousands who've been there to cheer the riders on their way up, and who are now cheering everyone on their way down.

There are overhung Scandinavians, Dutch in bright orange, French in fancy dress and, increasingly, Union Jacks as you make your way down. Any British fans always greet the BBC vehicle with a wave and a shout, which makes me feel pretty good I have to say. Once we're off the mountain we head for our overnight accommodation, which has usually been booked about halfway between that day and the next day's finish. It's essential to arrive in time for food, a glass of Belgian beer (other beer is available) and a glass of red wine, before going to bed and preparing to do it all over again.

I'd been prepared to stay in France for 48 hours or so, just until Simon was able to sort out his family problems and return to the team. Sadly for him this wasn't going to happen, and I remained with Phil and Graham for another fifteen days, all the way to Paris.

It was some way into the second week before I really knew that I'd be calling the winner on the Champs Elysees, and by then the doping curse which so often haunts the race had appeared again. On July 24th, which was a rest day, the day when you do your laundry and pray nothing untoward occurs, we'd been staying in an hotel called Sept Molles (Seven Mills) which is down amongst the foothills of the Pyrenees and is the one beacon of luxury the BBC Radio team is allowed during the three and a half weeks of the race. Normally the rest day is just that, but by July 24th Michael Rasmussen, who'd won that stage which we reported from our hotel, had taken over the Yellow Jersey, and was due to give the traditional leader's press conference in Pau.

Rasmussen was riding under a cloud, the cloud surrounding his whereabouts earlier in the year, when he missed a routine drugs test by claiming he was in Mexico with his wife. It later transpired that he was training in Italy, where he would have been able to comply with the testers, and had in fact been spotted by an Italian journalist called David Cassani. Rasmussen denied all this, but we had to go in case the balloon went up. It didn't, or at least it didn't at that exact moment.

Phil, Graham and I drove the 100 kilometres or so to Pau for the non-event of a press conference then drove back to Sept Molles, where we'd anticipated the best meal of the trip. As we pulled up in the hotel car park Phil Sheehan's mobile rang. It was the office to say that the Kazakh rider Alexander Vinoukorov had tested positive for blood doping, and that his Astana team had withdrawn for the race.

This was a big story, and one we had to react to instantly. Vinokourov was a major contender and this would be the biggest scandal since Strasbourg the previous year. Phil made the decision that we'd have to turn around and head back to Pau to see if anyone could comment on proceedings. I pointed out that someone needed to stay in the hotel to broadcast to the many outlets who'd be wanting to speak with us, and so out came the Comrex, and instead of enjoying the gentle ambience of our favourite hotel, I was in my room broadcasting about Vinokourov and Rasmussen whilst my poor colleagues were back on the road to Pau.

I hasten to add that we did eventually get to eat, and that over dinner we discussed what might happen next. We decided that for things to get any worse then our own Bradley Wiggins would have to be kicked off the race. I might add that as well as the Astana scandal, Iban Mayo of Spain had also tested positive on the rest day, so what did happen next was that the riders staged a protest at the start of the following stage over the organisers lax approach to drug testing, and we duly went to the town of Orthez and collected some very telling interviews from, amongst others, Britain's David Millar, once banned for two years for doping but now almost evangelical in his pursuit of a clean sport.

The stage on that Tuesday, July 25th, was won by Michael Rasmussen. After the stage news reached us that Cristian Moreni of Cofidis had tested positive, and that his team had withdrawn from the tour. This meant that we had indeed lost Bradley Wiggins, but we were unable to interview him since the team bus had driven off in the opposite direction.

We headed off to Toulouse, the second favourite stop-over after Sept Molles, and hoped for a quieter evening. We'd already had to field calls from every conceivable BBC outlet. I'd spoken to Jeremy Vine on Radio Two, Phil had had a blazing row with the *Today* programme and all we wanted to do was to sit down, eat and drink, admire the stunning women of Toulouse as they passed by our restaurant, and prepare for the following day's stage, which took the riders from Pau to Castelsarassin.

Now journalists on the road do enjoy a drink in the evening, and that night in Toulouse we felt we'd deserved another bottle of red wine as we sat in a prime position overlooking one of the big squares to be found in this most lovely of French cities. We knew we didn't have to start too early the following morning, so we'd even stayed up late. It was around about midnight when Phil's mobile rang. It was, of course, the office, with the news that Michael Rasmussen had been sacked by his Dutch Rabobank team and was out of the Tour de France. Since he was wearing the Yellow Jersey at this time, it was quite a major story to put it mildly.

Whatever programme was on the air at that time wanted immediate reaction. That meant that I had to speak to them as I walked up and down that open square in Toulouse, trying to sober up and remember the complexities of the Rasmussen case. I think I got away with it, but worse was to follow, since the *Breakfast Show* then wanted us on at the very start of their programme, at six o'clock the following morning.

Now no-one goes out eating and drinking late if they have

to be up early the following morning, unless they're very silly. We'd only done it because we weren't anticipating having to do so. Not so bright and early on that Wednesday Phil set up the Comrex in his room, and I put on the headphones to hear Nicky Campbell yawning. Once again I did the obligatory two-way, went for breakfast, came back to do the *Today* programme, and then set off to cover the stage, servicing whichever outlets wanted material as we went.

Fortunately that was the end of the scandal, at least for a while. The Spaniard Alberto Contador took the yellow jersey to Paris, and Michael Rasmussen was last heard of appearing on the Danish version of *Strictly Come Dancing*. Contador would later be stripped of his Tour de France wins after he tested positive.

The following year, 2008, I was given the job of all jobs. With Simon on duty at the European Football Championship Finals and then the Olympics in Beijing, I was to do the whole of the Tour de France. To make things even better, by 2008 two other things had happened. Firstly, Phil Sheehan and I had persuaded BBC Radio to broadcast the last hour of each stage live on the BBC website, and when cricket and tennis didn't take precedence, on BBC 5 Live Sports Extra. Secondly, British Cycling had produced a rider who was going to dramatically raise the profile of the sport at home, and particularly the profile of the Tour de France. We had a rider who, we hoped, might actually win a stage of the race. His name was Mark Cavendish, and in 2008 he came of age.

The 2008 race started in Brest in Brittany before heading eastwards across France, then south to the Pyrenees and finally into the Alps, with the dramatic ride up to Alpe d'Huez as the centrepiece. Mark Cavendish was hoping to at least manage a stage win, something few British riders had ever achieved before.

As the race snaked its way south and east, Cavendish failed to exploit the early opportunities given to the sprinters. Breakaways stayed away and the Norwegian Thor Hushovd and France's diminutive Samuel Dumoulins took wins we'd hoped the man from the Isle of Man might take.

By Wednesday July 9th we were in the town of Chateauroux, famous for its maximum security prison amongst other things, and the riders were making their way across the flatlands of central France from Cholet. There was a breakaway group, amongst whom was the Champion of France, Nicolas Vogondy, and as the race approached the finish, the sprinters were chasing this group down and in the commentary box I was becoming increasingly nervous.

Bearing in mind my previous experiences of calling home sprint finishes, where I generally took a deep breath and hoped for the best, I knew that on this occasion I could be describing history. If Cavendish won then my commentary would be used far and wide across the BBC, and future generations of producers would take this out of the sports archive to reflect on the first win by a potential champion.

As Cavendish's Columbia team piled on the pressure, Vogondy made a break for the line. In the box my commentary reflected this. I remember suggesting that our man might be denied again, just like he had been when Dumoulins stayed clear in Nantes two days previously. Then I saw the typical hunched style of the Manx Missile as he broke through on the left hand side of the course. He was being challenged by Hushovd, and in my enthusiasm I kept saying "Cavendish and Hushovd, Cavendish and Hushovd," then "Come on Cav," just as if I was a fan standing by the side of the road.

Perhaps it was unprofessional, but I felt I was simply doing what anyone else in my position would have done. I also had to make sure I called it right, because if I said Cavendish had won and he hadn't then the commentary would have been unusable. Even worse, if I said Cavendish hadn't won and he had, then my embarrassment would have been even greater.

Of course you don't think about this as the riders charge towards you, and I'm delighted to say that as they crossed the line I said "And Mark Cavendish wins Stage Five of the Tour de France here in Chateauroux. Fantastic."

Now there used to be a rule on the Tour de France that

anytime there was a British winner the BBC Radio team was entitled to a bottle of Champagne. I believe we did just that later that evening, but it had to stop because Cavendish wasn't content with winning just once. The following Saturday he won in the rain in Toulouse, where we were able to enjoy a night out with no scandal, just the problem of trying to find a laundry which was open on a Sunday. There were troubled times ahead, mainly involving an Italian rider called Ricardo Ricco, but our headlines all surrounded Cav.

By the time he won consecutive stages in Narbonne and Nimes the BBC commentary team had even become news, with French Radio standing behind our broadcasting position to record my description of another British victory. It was a far cry from the days when hardly any of our riders took part in the event, and we revelled in its significance.

Phil Sheehan had the job of going down to interview the riders, and Cavendish usually responded to a familiar British voice amongst all the foreign microphones desperate for a quote. I'd interviewed Mark at the start in Brest, and managed one more conversation with him, through a car window at the top of a mountain when he'd retired from the race and was preparing to go home and build up to the Olympic Games, where he was competing in The Madison alongside Bradley Wiggins.

By the time I did my next tour, in 2010, we were in Rotterdam, Cavendish had become a superstar and Wiggins had finished third overall. I spoke to both of them before the prologue time trial, but by then it was becoming harder and harder to get close. I had to use all my experience to manoeuvre myself next to Cavendish during the free for all which followed his team presentation in Holland, and it was even worse with Wiggins, who was having a most un-Bradley like strop on the day of the Team Sky launch, and wasn't giving any interviews at all. He did eventually speak to me, though only for a couple of minutes, and as the race headed off into Belgium and all points south I'd done my job.

By the time I handed over to Simon Brotherton after the first rest day, I'd called Cavendish home on a further two occasions, and Simon had the privilege of commentating on three more wins, including the final stage on the Champs Elysee. In 2011 Cavendish won another five stages and took the green points jersey, before capping it all by winning the world road race title in Copenhagen.

Then came 2012, the year Bradley Wiggins won in Paris. I covered the whole tour, first as a commentator, then as producer/interviewer. I called Wiggins home in the time trial which virtually confirmed him as victor, then I was on the Champs Elysee to interview both him and Cavendish on the greatest of all days for British cycling. Bradley in yellow, Mark winning in Paris again. Impossible to beat I reckon. It's a far cry from Operacion Puerta and the mayhem of 2006 where it all started for me. I'm still something of an outsider in the cycling world, but thanks to the generosity of Simon Brotherton for allowing me to be his deputy, and the unerring professionalism and driving ability of Graham Jones, I've had moments I'll never forget.

There have been other more forgettable moments though. We once lost Phil Sheehan in Montpelier when he went out jogging and couldn't find the hotel again. He was brought back by a couple of senior citizens who'd taken pity on him. We've acquired a satnav with the voice of Clint Eastwood which annoyed us so much we had to switch him off. We've eaten more baguettes than are good for us at the Tour buvette, and kept the Belgian beer industry in profit. I've also been spat at by a most unpleasant Australian cyclist called Skippy, who later chased me into a hotel in Italy threatening to beat me up.

Along the way we've had contributions from a Danish rider who once won a cow, from the legendary Marcel from Luxembourg who knows everything there is to know about the Schleck brothers, from Belgians, Austrians, Australians and the excellent Chris Boardman. We also call upon our colleagues in the British media who answer our requests and come and join us in the commentary box. As mentioned before, top of the list are the Fotheringham's and Steve Farrand, who were there at the start for me, and who've never let me down since.

The one thing we haven't had to do again is put the microphone next to the air conditioning unit because from a distance it sounds like a helicopter. But who knows what delights lie in store for me in the future?

20

"And Jimmy Glass Has Scored for Carlisle United!"

There are times when you turn up for work and history happens around you.

On May 8th 1999 I'd been sent to cover a game in Division Three, which used to be Division Four and is now League Two. Carlisle United were playing Plymouth Argyle in their final game of the season. They were bottom of the table, a point behind Scarborough, who were also at home, to Peterborough.

I've always had a soft spot for Carlisle United. One of my dearest friends in broadcasting was Derek Lacey, who covered them for many years home and away for BBC Cumbria. Derek was a Londoner, who arrived in Carlisle by mistake.

He'd been working for the Post Office on the mail trains, and one August night in 1963 he'd had to extend his stay in Carlisle, where his mail train terminated, because the line had been closed after the train travelling in the opposite direction had been involved in an "incident". The train Derek could have been on, if fate had decreed differently, had fallen victim to one of the most notorious crimes of the 20th century, The Great Train Robbery. It was during this enforced visit that he met the woman who was to become his wife, and so he stayed and became part of the fabric of the city.

Wherever you went in Carlisle, if you were with Derek it was like being with royalty. He was constantly being stopped by fans who wanted to know the latest news, and, of course, to answer the question "Do you think we'll win on Saturday Derek?"

Derek sadly passed away a couple of years ago, and I miss his constant cheerfulness. In the past four seasons before the Plymouth game he'd seen his team promoted, relegated, promoted again and relegated again. Now they were in extreme danger of falling through the league trapdoor altogether. To avoid that, they had to better Scarborough's result. Derek had covered all these events with his usual good humour.

This time around Carlisle's problems had been compounded by a goalkeeping crisis. Tony Caig, their regular keeper for many seasons, had been sold to Blackpool, and his replacement Richard Knight had had his loan spell cut short by injury. They'd had to get special dispensation from the Football League to bring in a replacement goalkeeper, and the man they'd chosen was Jimmy Glass.

Glass was signed on an emergency deal from Swindon Town. He'd let in three in his opening game at home to Darlington then had kept a clean sheet in a goalless draw at Hartlepool. This was to be his third and last game for Carlisle, and it was a game which would write the name of Jimmy Glass into local folklore.

I'd hoped to use one of BBC Cumbria's ISDN lines, but on arrival discovered that my equipment wouldn't connect to theirs. This meant that BBC 5 Live was in serious danger of not being able to report on the biggest game in Carlisle's recent history.

The only other ISDN in the ground belonged to the local commercial station CFM. Each ISDN has two connections, or "ports," as they're better known. CFM's second port was being used by the local commercial station from Plymouth. Their reporter was Graham Hambley, who doubled up as the correspondent of the local evening paper, The *Plymouth Evening Herald*.

I knew Graham slightly, because he'd appeared on a programme I'd produced about Plymouth Argyle's run to the FA Cup semi-final in 1984. That connection wouldn't do me any good unfortunately, since he had broadcasting commitments as well. However, when he looked into his bag, Graham discovered that he'd left a crucial piece of equipment behind. He couldn't broadcast and he didn't seem too concerned. "I'll just do it on the phone" was his reaction, since I don't think his station was entirely committed to covering Argyle.

Quick as a flash I turned to the commentator from CFM. If the BBC were to cross their palms with silver, would CFM allow me to use their second port? Graham was happy for me to do the deal, CFM was happy to take the money, and I was just relieved to actually be broadcasting.

Across the country my good friend Alan Biggs had been dispatched to the McCain Stadium for the Scarborough game. He vividly describes what happened at his end in his book *Confessions of a Football Reporter*. Here's what was occurring further north and west.

In the Carlisle programme, a copy of which I still have, autographed by Jimmy Glass, Nigel Pearson, in his "Coach Notes" column, points out that "There will no doubt be an abundance of radios at both grounds."

What those listening to BBC Radio 5 Live heard first of all was news of a goal for Peterborough. It was scored by Richard Scott after just seven minutes, and meant that if scores stayed the same then Carlisle would be staying up on goal difference. It stayed like that for 35 wonderful minutes, then just before half-time the ground was silenced as Scarborough's Darren Roberts equalised. Carlisle were now a point adrift, and needed to score. Since they'd lost the toss, they'd have to do it with the Warwick Road behind them, whereas they always preferred to attack that end in the second half.

Four minutes after the break all that seemed irrelevant. That was because Plymouth's Lee Phillips chose the moment to score his first ever league goal for the club. As things stood, Scarborough had 48 points, and Carlisle only 46.

It stayed that way until just past the hour mark, when Carlisle captain Ian Brightwell equalised. It lifted Carlisle's points total to 47, but that still wasn't enough to overhaul Scarborough. A proud record of more than 70 years in the Football League was about to come to an end.

Things remained unchanged until deep into Brunton Park stoppage time. By then Scarborough's game had already finished and Alan Biggs had told the nation that the Yorkshire club's fans were celebrating their survival. In Carlisle the biggest crowd of the season were in despair as their beloved club stood on the brink of not just relegation but removal from the Football League.

The fourth official had raised the numbers board, which showed that four minutes of stoppage time were to be played. My stopwatch told me we'd already played that when Carlisle won a corner on the right. I looked down at Nigel Pearson on the touchline. He waved to Jimmy Glass and told him to go up for the kick. Glass was wearing a red goalkeeper's jersey with black sleeves, Carlisle's players were in blue, Plymouth's in green. The corner came over and Carlisle's Scott Dobie headed goalwards. The Plymouth keeper punched the ball out and it fell straight to the feet of Glass, who crashed it into the net.

I can offer no better description of the event than to reproduce Derek Lacey's commentary.

"So ... deep, deep, deep, I make it 60 seconds. Jimmy Glass knocks it long. It comes now to Bagshaw. Bagshaw back to Anthony. Up to Stevens ... and the ball goes out now for a corner to Carlisle United – will they have time to take it? Referee looks at his watch ... and here comes Jimmy Glass! Carlisle United goalkeeper Jimmy Glass is coming up for the kick – everyone is going up ... there isn't one player in the Carlisle half! Well, well ... and the corner kick comes in ... and ... the goalkeeper's punch ... oh ... Jimmy Glass! Jimmy Glass! Jimmy Glass, the goalkeeper, has scored a goal for Carlisle United! There's a pitch invasion! There is a pitch invasion! The referee has been swamped – they're bouncing on the crossbar!"

Sometimes when a goal is scored you have to follow the celebrations to work out exactly who put the ball in the net. Not on this occasion you didn't. Glass was the only player in red, and he'd quite definitely hammered that shot past the Plymouth defence. My task then was to "buzz" the studio, using the ringer we have on all our ISDN units. As the call was answered I just said, "You won't believe what's just happened here, the goalkeeper's scored for Carlisle."

The next half hour was chaotic. Instead of being one of the also ran stories on *Sports Report*, I was the lead. I somehow had to write a well-crafted piece in about five minutes then scramble down through the mayhem to secure the interviews the programme needed. I was the eye of the storm.

Alan Biggs blames me for ruining his afternoon and the big escape story he didn't have. Jimmy Glass's goal ruined Scarborough's afternoon, their season, and their Football League career. Certainly they never returned to the land of the 92, and in 2007 the club was wound up. Go past the old ground now and it's all boarded up with overgrown grass and rusting stands. As I write, Carlisle are sitting safely in the third tier of English football, but that didn't happen because of Jimmy Glass.

You see Carlisle never learned. The following season they escaped on the final day, despite losing at Brighton. It was an afternoon when fortunes fluctuated again, but I was in Barcelona covering the Spanish Grand Prix, and watched my colleague Jonathan Legards suffering as his beloved Chester City were relegated instead.

The year after that they escaped with one game still to play. I was at Lincoln City's Sincil Bank to see that one, along with the ever smiling Lacey. Then something went wrong and they finished 17th, but in season 2002-3 things returned to normal. This time the stakes were even higher, because two sides were to be relegated instead of just one. Carlisle stayed up on the last day, despite losing at home to Bournemouth. Barnet and Exeter went down.

By now the club had been taken over by a genial Irishman called John Courtenay who appointed Roddy Collins, the brother of the boxer Steve, as his manager. John would join Derek and I on our occasional Friday nights out in the City, and so it came to pass that at the end of season 2003-04, five years after Jimmy Glass's heroics, the trapdoor finally opened and swallowed up The Cumbrians.

John Courtenay had appointed a Carlisle boy as his manager by now. His name was Paul Simpson, he'd enjoyed a decent playing career and had had some success as a manager at Rochdale. But by the time he arrived at Brunton Park in October the damage had already been done. Carlisle were rock bottom of the table, with just one win all season and by December 13th, 21 games into the campaign, they'd collected just five points. Nothing could save them

Simpson then took them on a remarkable journey, as they lost just three of their next 15 matches but they were coming back from an impossible situation, and on the penultimate day of the 2003-04 season they could only draw against Cheltenham, and down they went. On that afternoon it was John Courtenay who fronted up to speak live on *Sports Report*.

Simpson brought them straight back up. Not automatically of course, that would have been too easy. Instead, Carlisle had to go into a play-off semi-final against Aldershot, which they won after the most extraordinary penalty shoot-out I think I've ever seen. They then beat Stevenage 1-0 in the final, with a goal from Peter Murphy, who may not have been around when Jimmy Glass scored, but who had played enough games to become another Brunton Park legend. The following season, at Mansfield Town's Field Mill ground, Paul Simpson took them up again, and I'm delighted to say that I was there to see it. My only problem that day was dragging Paul away from the clutches of Derek, who was trying to conduct the longest interview in football history as my producer in London wanted to know where Simpson was and why wasn't he coming to talk to us.

As for Jimmy Glass, well if he hadn't gone up for that corner, then the most significant person of that name on Google would be an executed murderer from Louisiana. However, Glass's 15 seconds of fame mean he'll never have to buy a drink on Botchergate ever again.

I've spoken to Jimmy several times since then. He's now a taxi driver in Bournemouth, but whenever the call comes from the border city, he's only too happy to return. My one regret is that Derek Lacey is no longer there to watch. As I say, sometimes history just happens around you. Rest in Peace my friend.

"And Jimmy Glass, the goalkeeper has scored a goal for Carlisle United. There's a pitch invasion, there's a pitch invasion. They're bouncing on the crossbar."

DEREK LACEY 1942-2009

21

Slightly Sideways – Motor Bikes with No Brakes

When I moved from Newcastle to Ipswich in 1981, as part of my job I inherited the Ipswich Witches Speedway team. On Tyneside there had been the Newcastle Diamonds, but Charles had always gone to cover that down at the Brough Park Greyhound Track, and all I knew of the sport was that Newcastle had two riders called Owen – Tom and Joe, and later an Australian called Robbie Blackadder, long before Richard Curtis and Ben Elton created Rowan Atkinson's great comedy vehicle.

The Diamonds were a kind of add-on to North-East sport, and like the basketball and the ice hockey we had to give them due deference and report what was happening. Actually I quite enjoyed covering the basketball, and Alison and I would often go over to the Crowtree Leisure Centre on a Sunday evening to watch Sunderland's Division One team in action.

Basketball and ice hockey hardly registered in Suffolk, even Rugby Union was only played at a fairly low level. Speedway was another matter entirely. After Ipswich Town the Witches were the biggest news around. Their promoter when I arrived was John Berry, and John and I took an immediate liking to each other. He needed to put bodies through the turnstiles and Radio Orwell was one of the main outlets to let people know what was happening. This meant that he'd phone me with stories, and if I was short of a piece on my *Sportsdesk's* John would always find something to fill the space.

What was happening in early 1981 was that John Berry had

made some unpopular decisions in the transfer market. He'd allowed two of the club's top riders to move on, and the natives were restless. One was an Australian called Billy Sanders, who was later to return to Ipswich, and whose life ended tragically. The other was John Louis, Ipswich born and bred, and as much a part of the furniture as Bobby Robson was at Portman Road.

Replacing them were two Americans, Denis Sigalos and John Cook. Sigalos came with an excellent pedigree, which he was to fulfil by finishing third in the 1982 World Final in Los Angeles, behind the Golden Boy of the time, Bruce Penhall. Cook was an unknown quantity, but they both quickly started to rack up the points, and the crowd took to them.

I took to them as well. They shared digs in the suburb of Kesgrave, and I'd often pop over to speak to one or other of them to preview whichever meeting was coming up. The garage was always full of bits of speedway bikes and the atmosphere always informal. The team also included a likeable Dane called Preben Eriksen, who lived in the next village to me, and a couple of local boys, Kevin Jolly and Nigel Flatman.

Race night at Foxhall Stadium was Thursday, and I'd drive down the country lanes and through the trees to the track. My Radio Orwell car was always allocated a special parking place next to the pits, and I was able to walk in through the pit gate and across to our rather rudimentary commentary box, where Mike Ashby, Radio Orwell's accountant, would sit and watch and explain things, often over a couple of cans of cider.

I took to the sport pretty quickly, understanding terms like "paid maximums" and "rider replacement," and the informal press arrangements meant that I could interview anyone at any time. Often these took place in the changing rooms after the meeting, and it was there I got to know people like Penhall, Hans Nielsen and Erik Gundersen, all of whom would go on to become World Champions.

I developed other friendships, notably with Elvin King, Speedway Correspondent of the *Ipswich Evening Star*, and with James Easter, whose company "Travel Plus," was the leading provider for fans wishing to travel to major events both at home and abroad.

In 1983 Billy Sanders ended his exile and came back to Foxhall and in the autumn of that year he qualified for the World Final, which was to take place in Norden in West Germany, a place as remote as, say Wick would be in the United Kingdom.

That summer, James Easter and I had undertaken a fact finding mission, which basically meant we drank too much on the ferry, and he then spent hours scouring the towns and villages close to Norden looking for accommodation for September's final. He must have looked at every hotel room north of Bremen!

In September I drove to Norden with Elvin King, taking the ferry from Felixtowe to Zebrugge and then just heading north. We went through Belgium and Holland and eventually wound our way onto the north coast of Germany and our James Easter reserved hotel. Bruce Penhall later arrived in town having forgotten his passport, and having had to travel across the various border crossings in the boot of his manager's car.

On Friday evening I broadcast Radio Orwell's sports programme live from my hotel room, using a combination of crocodile clips and tangled wires to link up to my assistant Peter Robinson in the studio in Ipswich. On race day I commentated from my seat in a temporary stand (much of Norden was temporary) and Billy Sanders finished second behind Egon Muller, the home favourite who never came close to winning the title again. Billy was disappointed but had no reason to be.

The following season Ipswich won the league and cup double. James and I commentated on the deciding league fixture from the roof of the offices at Reading. Orwell ran a one hour documentary after that, with contributions from all the riders, and we even sold a few hundred commemorative cassette copies. Sanders and Kai Niemi reached the World Final, held in Gothenburg's Ullevi Stadium. Elvin and I made another epic journey north, by ferry and car to Sweden.

By now though I was considering my future, although before I finally left Foxhall behind, the team organised for me to ride a speedway bike, dressed in Nigel Flatman's leathers. These bikes have no brakes of course, and me being a coward, I became the only person in Ipswich speedway history to be overtaken by someone on the centre green, walking!

When the next years World Final came around, I was working for the BBC. In fact on one of my first football reporting assignments, at Portman Road towards the end of the 1984-85 campaign I received some dreadful news. Billy Sanders, the man I'd followed to two World Finals, the man who'd been the lynchpin of the Witches in my final two years in Suffolk, had been found dead in the woods near the stadium. He'd taken his own life. It was such a waste for someone who'd diced with death every time he took to the track.

Billy wasn't the only one to come to such a tragic end. One afternoon I was allowed into Ipswich Hospital to interview another rider who'd crashed during a meeting at Foxhall. His name was Kenny Carter, and he was a rough and ready Yorkshireman who was tipped to become Britain's next World Champion.

Kenny was in a spot of pain, but he spoke to me and I was grateful. A couple of years later he killed both his wife and himself in a bizarre shooting incident at his farm in the Yorkshire hills.

The 1985 World Final was being held in the UK, at the Odsal Stadium in Bradford. Radio 2 wasn't especially interested, but I persuaded them to put in an outside broadcast, and I employed Tony Millard, an ebullient commentator from Brighton, to cover the event as I produced from our little van parked somewhere on the outside of the track.

Erik Gundersen won his second World Title, at around about half past four on the Saturday, and I was told that *Sports Report* would take a package from Tony, to include an interview with Gundersen as part of it. Off I went down to the pits, only to discover that Gundersen was nowhere to be found. He was in fact in the Doping Control Room, trying hard to produce a urine sample.

There then followed a major stand-off between myself

and speedway's officialdom. There hadn't been any live TV coverage, and I'd had to fight hard to persuade my editor to let us come to Bradford. I wasn't going to fail now. I could see Erik and he could see me. He wanted to come and talk, but until he'd done what he had to do, then the jobsworth wouldn't let him. Eventually sense prevailed and a helpful British official, conscious of the bad publicity this would give to speedway, allowed me to congratulate one of speedway's nice guys on winning the title. And yes, it did make *Sports Report*. I was very proud.

Later on, at the same track, Erik Gundersen nearly lost his life at a World Team Cup Final, when he was hit from behind by another rider. He never sat on a bike again, but was able to return to the sport as team manager for the Danish national squad.

It would be another five years before I went to my next World Final. I suppose I'd become busy developing my BBC Career, and it had kind of passed me by. This meeting was, once again, at Odsal, and it was won by the Swede Per Jonsson. It remains the most exciting speedway meeting I'd ever seen, and it re-awakened my interest.

The BBC had by now started a sports programme on a Sunday afternoon, and I convinced them that it would be a good idea to broadcast some of the major speedway events as part of that show. We started with the British Final, held at Coventry, and I remember spending time with Coventry promoter Charles Ochiltree negotiating access for my BBC van and me. Once again, Millard did the commentating, and I did the interviews. At that time the top British rider was Simon Wigg (another rider who died tragically young), and he was thrilled that the BBC had come calling, as were the speedway press. They even invited me to their pre-British Final lunches from then on, always held in Coventry, usually with the great Barry Briggs in attendance.

In all I went to another three World Finals, after help from Charles Runcie, a good friend from our days together at Radio Orwell. Charles was now head of sport for the English regions, and he managed to organise funding whereby I interviewed all the various riders for their local radio stations, and the stations made a contribution.

My final World Final, indeed the last one before Ole Olsen masterminded the Grand Prix series which has taken speedway into the 21st century, was in Vojens in Denmark in 1994. Two British riders were taking part, they were Mark Loram and Chris Louis, who were brothers-in-law. It was a prefect piece for *Sport on Four*, and It meant I had to go and interview them both. As luck would have it, both were taking part in a meeting at Foxhall one Thursday night.

So it came to pass that nearly a decade after I'd left, I returned to the track where I'd enjoyed myself so much during the early 1980s. I was greeted enthusiastically, and the centre green announcer even interviewed me about the feature I was making. Best of all, up in the ramshackle commentary box, Mike Ashby had turned up, and had brought a couple of cans of cider.

Now I keep in touch with the sport through *Speedway Star*, magazine. I'm on their mailing list and never wish to be taken off, as how else can I read Elvin King's news of the Witches. I also watch the Grands Prix on Eurosport, and marvel how they manage to ride those bikes, 500cc, and no brakes. I know I couldn't, after all I tried it once!

22

Woke Up, Had Breakfast, Interviewed Dull Scot (Colin McRae and the World Rally Championship)

Phil Sheehan and I were in Glasgow on a September Saturday in 2008, driving back to our hotel after the final stage of the Tour of Britain Cycle Race when we heard the news on the radio. There'd been a helicopter crash, and unconfirmed reports said that amongst the victims was the former World Rally Champion, Colin McRae. Colin didn't drive any more, of course, but he'd made a fortune by breaking the Scandinavian domination of the sport throughout the late 1990s and the early part of the New Millennium.

To Phil, McRae's passing meant little or nothing, but for me it closed an important chapter of my life, one which had begun 17 years earlier, and which, like Formula One, had taken me to some places I'd never have dreamed of. It had also allowed me to witness at first hand the media development of a genuine sporting superstar.

Back in the summer of 1991, Bob Shennan, recently appointed sports editor of BBC Radio, had called me and asked if I'd produce our coverage of the RAC Rally for that year. This meant working in our studio in Harrogate as reporter Andy Smith did regular voice reports for the station whilst the drivers raced the length and breadth of the country, watched by hundreds of thousands of enthusiasts, who crowded the forests and stately homes to watch the cars hurtle through.

That year there was hardly a British driver to trouble the scorers, as Juha Kankkunen of Finland took the title yet again. However, out on the road something interesting had happened. Whereas previously we'd never been able to hear from the drivers during the event, now we could.

This was because a month or so before the event I'd been put in touch with a rally enthusiast (and boy, could those guys be enthusiastic) named Steve Dewitt. Steve presented the early breakfast show on Radio Wales and was offering to interview drivers on the road and send the interviews back to the studio. All he wanted in return was a vehicle pass and accreditation for himself and his navigator, a young Welshman called Nigel Nelson.

As the week went by two things became apparent to me. Firstly Steve Dewitt's interviews weren't particularly good, too much of the fan with the microphone, secondly, he did manage to be in the right place at the right time to actually do them.

The following year we were in Chester, and I'd been given something of a free role. I'd recorded some stuff on the opening day and had then been left with little to do. So I went out into the field, and met up with Steve and Nigel in Keilder Forest. We'd had a similar service to the previous year, interviews delivered on time but of no real substance, and I wanted to try and change that. So in Keilder I sent Steve off in one direction and told Nigel to jump in with me. By the end of the evening we'd interviewed a rally team chief, set up an interview for the *Today Programme*, and caught up with the overnight leader somewhere near Carlisle Airport. Significantly, wherever I wanted to go, Nigel made sure we arrived. Before we parted in Chester he gave me his card.

The following year we dispensed with Dewitt but kept his navigator, and instead Nigel, who by then was a constable with Dyffed Powys police, set off on the road with me. I loved planning the logistics of the event, of where we needed to be in order to send material back. With so much new technology coming through I discovered ISDN's in church halls, gift shops and the National Trust HQ in Windermere. My BBC car was even rigged up with equipment allowing us to send telephone quality interviews and reports when we could find a signal. These were the very early days of mobile phones and they were also the early days of two very special British rally drivers. Both would become World Champions.

One was a tall, sandy haired kid from Oxford, Richard Burns, cruelly taken by a brain tumour at a very early age; the other was the moody, taciturn McRae. Nigel and I pursued them through the country homes of Sunday, to the forests of Wales and Northumberland. Nigel seemed to know exactly where each team would have their intermediate service halts (usually in a farmyard or round the back of a motor dealer), and there we'd find the drivers. We tried to limit our interviews with Colin to one a day, mainly because he simply didn't like doing them. Fortunately his co-driver Nicky Grist could talk for Wales, and team principal David Richards was always anxious to please.

Over time Colin grew to tolerate, rather than like us. In 1993 we were on hand in Keilder when a tree branch went through his radiator and he had to retire. I did the interview and Nigel and I raced back to Carlisle to send the stuff. It was the lead on the sports desks but as we were sending, Graham Taylor was sacked as England football manager, and we were stood down for the rest of the day. We ended up in an Indian restaurant in Newcastle at a table next to Andy Cole. Nigel didn't know who he was.

We caught up with Colin in 1994 when he became the first British winner of his home event since Roger Clarke in 1976. The following year he took the World Title and Nigel and I battled through the snow to catch up with him in mid-Wales, sending the interview back, only to listen, and listen and listen, to then find out that the producer of the 5 Live Programme didn't think it important enough, so she didn't use it. It was a world exclusive by the way, just thought I'd mention it, the first interview with the first ever British World Rally Champion!

The rally always started early, and breakfast in the media

hotels was usually a quiet affair, with just the TV and radio crews wishing they were somewhere else, like still in bed. It was there that Andrew Williams, a BBC TV producer, came up with the phrase to describe my day: "Woke up, had breakfast, interviewed dour Scot".

In December 1996, just after I'd been given the Formula One pit lane reporters job, Andrew called me. He needed someone to do a job, and wondered if I could help him out. I enquired what the job might be, and he stunned me by saying, "I need someone to do the interviews on the Monte Carlo Rally, it's the third week in January, do you think you could manage it?"

I cleared it with Gordon Turnbull and in January I was on the plane with the TV crew, and off to Nice. Andrew produced, the editor was a bespectacled extrovert from Pebble Mill by the name of Phil Thickett, and there was my interview team, a cameraman called Jim and Gordon the sound recordist. They would be my eyes and ears.

Monte Carlo went well. We even managed to beat Italian TV to the first interview with the winner, an Italian called Pierro Liatti. Back in the hotel Phil and Andrew asked me if I'd like to join the crew for the rest of the season. They knew of my F1 commitments, and had another reporter, Jeremy Hart, who'd do half of the events. So I opened my diary, and tried to plot what was to become the most amazing year of my working life.

In March I flew from Birmingham to Nairobi for the Safari Rally, then down to Melbourne for the Grand Prix. Later in the year I went from Athens to Montreal via Heathrow, from Auckland back to London and then onto Budapest. In Corsica and San Remo, in New Zealand and then in Western Australia, where Tommy Makkinen won the World Title, I was there with Jim and Gordon, making sure we had the right men at the right time, and they included Colin McRae and Richard Burns.

One year I was given the task of talking to Richard Burns live on BBC 2 during the British Rally, now sponsored by Network Q. We were in a Cattle Market in Llandrindod Wells, and the idea was for Steve Rider to introduce the show from

Rally HQ, then hand over to me, where we had the broken oil filter which had caused Burns problems that day, and I was to discuss that with him.

The programme started and I was in position, but we had a problem, which was that Richard was nowhere to be seen. He'd been delayed at some control point on the way into the service park, but, we were told, he was on his way. Steve Rider handed to me. This was my first ever live TV broadcast and my interviewee wasn't there. Fortunately we had another piece of business to talk about. Colin McRae had had to retire, and I cued in 90 seconds of VT with him being interviewed about it.

As the piece started I looked around in blind panic. We still had no-one to talk to. Then a tall, gangling figure appeared from the far side of the cattle shed. I'd never been more pleased to see anyone than I was to see Richard Burns that Monday night.

I was later able to interview Richard live on TV when he became World Champion in 2001. I was also given the task of talking to Finland's Marcus Gronholm live on BBC 2 when he won the crown for the first time. The deal was that as his car pulled up, he'd get out and talk to me. A sterile area had been created around the car to stop other crews and fans from invading, and it should have been easy.

The director cued to me, and as he did Gronholm vanished under the weight of two gate crashers, who'd somehow evaded security and spoiled my interview. For a moment I didn't quite know what to say. They'd come from behind me and were now hoisting Marcus aloft. It was then that I recognised the invaders. Tommy Makkinen and Juha Kankkunen, the last two Finns to win the World Title were there to congratulate their fellow countryman. So, in fact, after a second or two of mayhem I had three World Champions to speak to. Not bad.

At the end of 1997 Bob Shennan had called to offer me a freelance contract to do Football and F1 for 5 Live, so that I could negotiate a fee for my rallying commitments. He'd heard me do commentary for TV on the "Super Special" stages in Silverstone and at Blenheim Palace, and I knew that BBC TV were angling for a new contract, and that I'd be one of their presenters if that happened. It didn't because Dave Richards sold the rights to Channel Four, so my decision to say to Bob: "Let's stay as we are for twelve months and then re-assess" had been justified.

Nigel and I battled on doing our radio stuff for a little while longer, but interest in the sport was starting to wane. With McRae and Burns no longer at the forefront, the British public weren't as keen, and with the decision to move the rally down to South Wales, much of the country felt excluded. That mad week in November, when hordes in anoraks and woolly hats would disappear into the forests now seemed like a moment of ancient history. Communications have improved so much that the challenge of trying to find the drivers and then find somewhere from which to send material has also diminished.

Nigel and I had experienced temperatures of minus 10 in Mid-Wales, where it was so cold my tape recorder froze. We nearly hit a tractor head on in Yorkshire, and conducted several broadcasts from peoples' front rooms, simply by knocking on the door and saying: "Hello, we're from the BBC, can we use your telephone?", something which worked every time. We've been frustrated and we've argued like an old married couple, but when we returned to Rally HQ after our five days on the road it was one of the most satisfying feelings I've ever experienced. We'd done a good job.

I covered my last Rally in 2004, spending the entire time in a dismal car park on the outskirts of Swansea. No-one wanted interviews any more, just updates into the sports desks as and when. The excitement of covering it had gone for me. The premature death of Richard Burns in November 2005 was a terrible blow, and with the passing of Colin McRae the Golden Age was consigned to history. At least I'd been there to enjoy some of it, and it was fun, even interviewing the Dour Scot.

23

Flying Down to Rio … What Happened Next

I mentioned earlier in the book that in 2012 I left the BBC after accepting a redundancy offer. At first I was terrified, having been in gainful employment all my life and never having had to offer myself on the open market, rather like one of those labourers at a Thomas Hardy hiring fair, or a docker working "The Lump".

Five years on it seems to have worked out pretty well. I still turn up and report for 5 Live or *Final Score* on a Saturday, I've been teaching at a couple of universities, and in the Summer of 2016 I did something I'd never done before, I found a job working at the Olympic Games.

The Olympics had never been on my radar before I "retired". I was either tied up with the football season or the next Formula One race. When I first joined Metro back in 1976, the Montreal Games were about to begin and we followed Brendan Foster's progress with interest. Four years later I recorded an in depth interview with a precocious 16-year-old about to go to his first games, a young man who later came and did work experience at the station. His name was Steve Cram and I'd like to think we taught him all he knows about broadcasting.

I was able to interview many other Olympic stars over the years of course. At Gateshead Stadium athletics events, great athletes like Ed Moses and Sebastian Coe would give their time to the young man from the local radio station. Then when I joined the BBC, I actually employed medal-winners like swimmer Anita Lonsbrough and show jumper David Broome as summarisers. It was always a thrill to meet these people, sometimes under strange circumstances. During the Monaco Grand Prix, I was dispatched to a black tie awards ceremony and ended up interviewing our greatest ever Olympian Steve Redgrave about who would play him in a film. I once spoke to Daley Thompson in the gents' changing room of an Ipswich clothes shop, and on another occasion tried very hard to persuade Linford Christie to speak to me during an athletics meeting in Cardiff. He declined.

In the early 1990s I came as close to the games as I thought I ever would. Manchester had bid for the honour of hosting the Olympics of the millennium and I was sent to Monaco to cover the final decision. My luggage failed to join me so I spent most of the time clad in Manchester Olympic Bid clothing, generously provided for me by the British Olympic Committee press office. On the morning of the announcement, the cyclist Chris Boardman came and did the breakfast show run, Radio 4 and 5 Live and impressed me as one of the most intelligent and forthright sportsmen I'd ever met. Little did I know that in years to come our paths would cross on the Tour de France. I also came upon the leader of Manchester City Council, one Graham Stringer, who tried and failed to remember that I was once a thorn in his side on the Student Representative Council at Sheffield University.

Sydney won the bid, Manchester was later awarded the Commonwealth Games, the legacy of which included a brand new football stadium for Manchester City and the velodrome which has been the hub for our track cyclists, many of whom, of course, I came across during my time covering events in places like Copenhagen and, as mentioned previously, Pruskowa. Bob Scott, the leader of the bid, was awarded a knighthood, my dealings with the games never progressed.

Sometime in 2012, I had a conversation with a colleague of mine, David Easson. Dave's a Scouser who lives in Sheffield and we'd laboured together on many occasions at press conferences and in post-match football scrums.

Dave had just returned from working at something called

the Youth Winter Olympics in Austria. It was an event I'd never heard of but he'd gone there to work as part of an Electronic News Gathering (ENG) crew for an organisation called the Olympic Broadcasting Service (OBS). The work sounded fun, the money was good and I wondered if this was something a new freelance might investigate. Better still, the man to contact was Grant Coleman, who was someone I'd known when he worked at the BBC in Southampton and who was now head of the Olympic News Channel which was part of OBS.

I sent off an email to Grant sometime in 2013, wondering if I might be someone he'd be interested in employing. The email I received back simply thanked me for my interest and said that if they were interested in me they'd be in touch, otherwise I wouldn't be hearing anything.

I put this one on the back burner and carried on with what freelance work I could pick up, whilst also enjoying the new freedom of being semi-retired. I finished the original version of this book in 2013 and started travelling around speaking to various groups about it which is where many people bought, and continued to buy a copy; a fact which delights both myself and my publisher. In 2014, Alison and I caught a little of the Winter Games in Sochi while travelling in Australia and New Zealand, then sometime in late 2014 I received an email from Grant. It simply asked me if I would be interested in being considered to work as a freelance at the Rio Olympic Games in the summer of 2016. I was invited to send in my CV.

This I duly did and within weeks I'd received the offer of employment for the Olympic News Channel. The job description was to work as a segment reporter for five weeks before and during the Rio Games. It was too good an offer to turn down. The email warned me that this wasn't a holiday and that I'd end up seeing less of the games than I would if I'd been at home. This didn't bother me in the slightest since I'd been to World Cups before and knew that if you were there to work then that was what you did. I also calculated that a month's employment would help provide me with the resources to plan our next "big" trip to Southern Africa, which we duly completed in early 2017.

As more information filtered through, I gained some sort of idea about who I'd be working with. I had lunch with David Easson in Sheffield and he filled me in about those I'd be working for. Grant Coleman was in charge and Chris van Schaick was his deputy. These were both people I'd come across during my broadcasting career. When the list of the other reporters was issued, there were plenty of familiar names, including several who worked alongside me on *Final Score* and 5 Live. I knew that whatever happened, and however hard the work was, it would be fun.

I signed the contract and sent it off and gradually OBS sent me more information. I discovered that I'd be covering the basketball tournament and so set to work learning about the various countries who'd qualified and which of the NBA superstars would be representing the USA. Details came through about our accommodation which seemed to be within walking distance of the International Broadcast Centre (IBC) where we'd be based. They even sent a rooming list where I discovered that I'd be sharing an apartment with *North-West Tonight's* sports reporter Richard Askam, someone I knew from my Saturday afternoon football shifts. It all seemed to be working towards an enjoyable month.

Richard had worked for OBS before, so I went across to Salford one day to meet up and sort out important things – like who was going to bring the tea bags and what he expected conditions to be like. All this was most useful when, in late July, Alison took me to our little local railway station and I set off on the journey to Rio, via Manchester and Lisbon.

I sat next to the coach of the Polish windsurfing team on the flight from Portugal to Brazil. When we arrived in Rio we were given our accreditation at the airport, and then Richard and I joined another couple of segment reporters for the journey across town to our home for the next month. We were housed in a complex of tower blocks with gardens, a swimming pool, a jogging track and a gym, which was much better than we could have hoped for. Richard and I were on the 14th floor with an open view from our balcony, each with our own bedroom and bathroom plus a communal living area. I mention all this because the standard of some accommodation in other parts of the city left a lot to be desired. There were tales of crews turning up to find their places unfinished and others who were miles from where they had to work. Not so for us.

We arrived on a Sunday and were due to start work on Monday with a number of familiarisation sessions. So on that first day, Richard and I took the bus out to our nearest beach and, as we watched the Atlantic waves roll in, I couldn't quite believe that in my retirement I was enjoying a completely new experience. That night, in the bar below our apartment, the rest of the crew began to arrive. There were familiar faces from my BBC days and some new people from different countries who I'd soon get to know much better. It was a first night party and, of course, completely unlike what was to follow.

What was to follow came at times as a shock to the system. At the start we had to work every day, 10 hour shifts, with different start and finish times – occasionally eight o'clock until six, then ten o'clock until eight. This was for research and preparation then making sense of features filmed by the ENG crews before the games started.

Working for the OBS at the Olympic Games isn't glamorous, but then I knew that before I arrived. There were certain things I didn't like: The IBC was a vast warehouse with massive double doors to keep intruders out. The catering facilities – offered by a company called Kilo – consisted of a hot buffet which was then weighed before you were charged. Trouble was, by the time you'd queued your food was cold, not helped by a ferocious air conditioning system in the refectory.

Once the games began my days became routine. I'd arrive around four o'clock in the afternoon and then prepare for the two basketball games I had to watch and edit. I'd do this as the games were in progress and edit them down before writing a voice track to match the pictures. Grant was insistent that our scripts should be as bland as possible with our notional target audience someone called Angus who lived in Bolivia and who knew little or nothing about the sport he was watching. That was who we were supplying packages to, those countries around the world who didn't have their own crews at events or who simply couldn't afford to be there.

We were all assigned to a picture editor, who worked in an editing booth next to our cavernous office. Once again I struck lucky, working with the force of nature who is TJ Jeffrey, a cheerful Englishwoman with whom I immediately felt at home. Apart from being a lovely person, she was just about the best editor in the place and she made my features come to life. We survived on a diet of tea and chocolate and were never downhearted, even at two o'clock in the morning as we tried to distil the latest cliffhanger between Nigeria and China. We both fell for the mad coach of the Venezuelan national team and marvelled at the skill of players like Spain's Pau Gasol and Kevin Durant of the USA. We were also blessed by having the best ENG crew around, marshalled by Jeff "Steely" Danzler, a basketball nut who knew what questions to ask post-match.

The efficiency of TJ and Jeff meant that when our final pieces were ready, and Chris van Schaick or the other scrutineers came to approve them, we hardly ever had to make any revisions. On the final day of the games, my men's final was the last event to finish but we managed to cut that in time. And at the end of it all I had a feeling of great satisfaction, overcoming even the night my evening meal consisted of a tin of sardines eaten in the corridor.

At the Olympic Games you're likely to meet famous people. One of my colleagues breezed in one morning to say he'd been talking to Michael Johnson in the security queue (I'm not going to go on about the security queue, the memory is still too raw!) I just kept meeting people from my past like the commentator from YLE in Finland who used to sit next to me in my Formula One days, or Nick Spencer who I'd last seen when we hired a car in Reykjavik and went off to see Iceland's Golden Falls.

There were plenty of BBC people working in the OBS offices and plenty of other BBC people working for … well the BBC of course. It was like a home from home in so many ways but my only "star spotting" moment came when I found myself in the lift with Lars Lagerback who'd just finished managing the Iceland football team in the European Championship Finals. They'd beaten England in one of our most humiliating defeats. I recognized him and said tongue in cheek, "Here I am in a lift with the most hated man in England." He smiled, and simply said ... "Harsh." As we exited onto the third floor I did congratulate him and suggested he must have been very proud of what he'd done in France. It was another classic occasion of me meeting someone famous who won't have a clue who I am.

I have few photographs of the trip mainly because my phone chose to break on the first day but also because we simply didn't get the chance to see any of Rio's many landmarks. I did make it to Corcovado where the statue of Christ dominates the skyline. It was a Sunday morning and I shared the experience with four other "segs", the tennis player Anna Ivanovic and the entire Australian women's synchronised swimming team.

By the end I suppose I was counting the days and the last night party was spoiled by the fact that we had a five o'clock start the following morning. I spent too much time with Jeff Danzler and had to be woken by Richard to catch the bus to take us to the airport. Many hours and several time zones later I found myself on the little train from Manchester to the Hope Valley, coincidentally sitting next to Tim Hammond, my one time assignment editor who I'd helped re-settle when he moved to Salford from London. As we talked about Rio, other passengers joined in envious of the experience I'd enjoyed. Whether they would have been happy with the cold food, the long and unsocial hours and the lack of tourist opportunities I wonder.

Months later, all those relative hardships are forgotten. From time to time I come across other Rio survivors and there are sincere embraces all round. I must have enjoyed it because at the start of 2017, whilst in South Africa, I received an email from Grant Coleman. It asked me if I would like to be considered for work at the 2018 Winter Games in South Korea. I'm going!

24

A-Z – An Alphabetical List of Others I Have Met

ATKINSON, Ron

Always a fabulous interviewee. After Sheffield Wednesday won the League Cup in 1991, I was asked to find out where he'd be the following morning as the *Breakfast Show* wanted to speak to him. He gave me the cheekiest of grins, and told me, in no uncertain terms, what I could do with the request. He'd still be out partying.

BEST, George

I interviewed him once, in one of the rooms off the tunnel at Nottingham Forest, probably before a Manchester United game. He couldn't have been more helpful. I thought he came across as something of a little boy lost, but the stories of how he treated people when he'd had a few show a different side to his character.

COWDREY, Colin

I once took afternoon tea with probably the greatest cricketer of his generation. He was in Chester-le-Street and whoever he was with invited me down to talk to the great man. As you would expect he was a perfect gentleman. I don't interview many cricketers, although my car journey with Geoffrey Boycott on the eve of the 1979 general election had its moments.

DAVIES, Sharon

I don't have the opportunity to interview many female sports stars, so I always remember having a chat with the one time Olympic swimmer. We spoke in my Datsun Sunny, because the acoustics in a car are always very good. I once passed her on the M1, her car registration was 15WIM. I waved, she didn't wave back. Women eh!

ECCLESTONE, Bernie

Bernard Charles Ecclestone remains, without a doubt, the hardest man I've ever had to interview. If he wanted to put his point across he was articulate, if he didn't want to talk, then he gave you closed answers all the time, sometimes very short ones at that. Few people used to frighten me, but Bernie did.

FRANCIS, Trevor

After Sheffield Wednesday lost the 1993 FA Cup Final with the last kick of extra time, someone had to go and interview their manager. I found Trevor sitting in the front seat of the team bus, down in the Wembley tunnel, looking like his footballing world had just collapsed, which I suppose in a way it had. The press corps was waiting, so I suggested that if I could persuade him to come out, then we'd do just one interview for all of us, which I'd start. There were no press officers in those days, so I just had to go and do it myself.

Trevor came down and spoke, although his heart must have been breaking. I always respected him for that, and we've remained friends ever since, always stopping for a cup of tea and a chat should our paths cross in various press rooms.

GIBSON, Steve

The man who saved Middlesbrough Football Club has never lost his love for the team. I have one image of him, standing on the running track at the old Wembley as the players came out before one of Boro's Cup Finals. He could have been in the Royal Box, but this was where he wanted to be. The look on his face said it all, pride, wonderment, like a schoolboy who'd won the golden ticket.

It was then that I felt privileged to be in a similar position. If you ever go to the Riverside, or to the Rockcliffe Park Training Ground, take a look at the picture of Gibson being thrown in the air by his players after they'd won the League Cup and you'll understand what real joy means.

HOLLOWAY, Ian

Ollie is marvellous, and a journalists dream. It was even worth braving the winter wind off the Irish Sea to travel to Blackpool and hear his words of wisdom. There is a snag, though, and it's trying to shut him up. He once gave me an answer which was five minutes 38 seconds long. Try editing that for your sports desk. Despite all that we love him.

IRVINE, Eddie

I've mentioned him briefly after his little contretemps with Johnny Herbert in Melbourne back in 1997, but Eddie was one of the shrewdest cookies on the block. He made a fortune out of property, had his choice of an array of beautiful women, and a mind which was sharp as a tack. What I also liked about him was that his mum and dad used to follow him around Europe in their camper van, staying on the fans campsites before coming into the paddock to mingle with the great and the bad.

JAY KAY of Jamiroquai

The Cat with the Hat, like Ruud Gullit was much taller than I expected. He's a self-confessed petrol head and came to the F1 races when he had a chance. I once looked on with him as Jonathan Legard walked backwards down the paddock, interviewing as he went. I told Jamiroquai's front man that we did special classes in interviewing whilst walking backwards. I think he actually believed me for a moment. Better talker than Ozzie Osbourne obviously.

KEANE, Roy

Once you're past the scary eyes and the fearsome reputation, Roy Keane is as good an interviewee as anyone. I saw him make his Nottingham Forest debut at Anfield, I interviewed him when he signed for Manchester United, and, most nerve-wracking of all, after his Ipswich side had thrown away a two goal lead in the last few moments at Sheffield United. He never let you down and he always gave you an honest answer to an honest question, quite at odds with his public persona.

LEE, Francis

I once turned up at his house in the Manchester suburbs, with Brian Clarke from Piccadilly Radio. Franny was chairman of Manchester City and he'd just sacked one of his managers (it was either Alan Ball or Brian Horton).

He opened the door, invited us in, was extremely friendly, but refused to give us an interview. He didn't relent! That was a rare occasion, of course, and he had his reasons.

McCARTHY, Mick

My favourite Mick-isms? How long do you have? On winning promotion with Sunderland: "I've got a smile like an upside down coat hanger!" After being pressed a little too hard by a journalist at a Wolves press conference: "We could carry on dancing round our handbags all night, and I'm still not going to tell you anything." A top, top bloke.

NEVILLE, Gary

Not every journalist's cup of tea, he once promised to give me an interview in the tunnel in Cardiff after Manchester United beat Wigan to win the League Cup. I waited and waited as the celebrations continued in the United dressing room. This was during the Fergie ban, and we desperately needed something from the winners. With about five minutes left on the programme Gary appeared, walked over and, good as his word, gave me a wonderfully honest appraisal of United's season. Mind you, his brother's just as good a talker.

O'NEILL, Martin

At the Football Writers Dinner in 1987, Martin O'Neill, recently retired footballer and now one of my summarisers had come along as a BBC guest. Unfortunately he'd forgotten to book a hotel room, and was desperately looking for somewhere to sleep. I happened to have a spare bed in my room, so he bunked down with me. At breakfast he told me that the chairman of Scunthorpe United had approached him with a view to becoming their next manager. He wanted to know my opinion and I told him to take the chance whilst there was one on the table because in 12 months time he'd just be another ex-footballer looking for a job. He didn't take my advice, and look what happened!

PLEAT, David

Arguably the best summariser I ever employed, and still at the top of his game. I remember being on the gantry at Southampton and handing out the tea. I'd brought four cups which my children had been using. Did the Tottenham manager want Mr Crocodile or Mr Giraffe? I think he settled for the former.

QUAX, Dick

New Zealand middle distance runner who came to race at Gateshead International Stadium in the late 1970s as Brendan Foster brought the best in the world to the North-East. I famously interviewed him as he was putting his tracksuit on, which meant I had to go up and down as he completed the job. I'm sure the exercise did me good.

ROSKO, Emperor

Not a real emperor of course, but a Radio One DJ when I caught up with him at Sheffield University in my student radio days. He was very, very full of himself, and halfway through one answer, did at least have the sense to say, "I've forgotten what the question was". So have I, so have I.

SMITH, "Jinky" Jim

My Newcastle United hero when I used to watch from the

terraces. After a knee injury finished his professional career he made a comeback playing for Whitley Bay in the Northern League. I was sent down to speak to him after the game and was told he'd see me in the dressing room.

Everyone else had gone by then and the only other person in the room was this rather shambling figure almost hiding in the corner. If I was nervous about meeting him then he was doubly so about speaking to me. The interview wasn't very good, he talked with his feet. Moral, you should never meet your heroes, they'll only disappoint.

THOMPSON, Daley

My interview with one of our most famous Olympians was remarkable because it took place in the changing room of a gentleman's outfitters in Ipswich. We even drew the curtains to maintain privacy. I bought a branded waterproof in the shop, which I still have 30 years later.

UTTLEY, Roger

When I was at Metro Radio in Newcastle, Roger Uttley was captain of the England Rugby Union team. During the Five Nations tournament, whenever the team was announced I'd head off to Killingworth, where he was a PE teacher, to speak to him. We usually did the interview by the side of a sports field as Year 9 pupils tried to impress him. The whole Independent Radio Network gladly took every piece, which was one of the reasons Mike Lewis took notice of me and later gave me a job.

VIDUKA, Mark

The only Australian I've ever met who knows nothing about cricket. Once at Middlesbrough's training ground I asked him for a comment about the news that Shane Warne had retired from the game that very day. "No interest at all, Mate" he said, and then offered some help, "Go and ask Mark Schwarzer." So I did, and he was very good.

WILKINSON, Howard

Fellow graduate of Sheffield University, and someone I've known for many years. After Leeds United won the title in 1992, when Manchester United failed to beat Liverpool, I went round to his house in the west end of Sheffield, completely unannounced, seeking an interview. He let me in and I was witness to the embarrassing interview which ITV managed to scramble together with Howard on the telephone before disappearing from view, never to show live top flight football again.

We then had to find a room to do our interview in, but the phone kept ringing, so we ended up in his downstairs toilet with the door closed. He ended the interview with the words, "I'm gob smacked." That interview went everywhere.

XAVIER, Abel

The man who looked like King Neptune with one of the silliest haircuts ever to grace a football field. I'm sure I interviewed him once, at either Liverpool or Everton, but how many other people do you know whose surnames begin with the letter X?

YALLOP, Frank

One pre-season in the early 1980s, Ipswich Town had played at Huddersfield on a Saturday, and stayed up in the north to take on Hull City on a Monday night. I'd been to the first game, then I'd returned home, before travelling back to Yorkshire.

On the Monday morning I received an emergency call from Pat Godbold at Portman Road. Could I come and take Paul Cooper's spare boots up to Hull please, and also, could I give a lift to a young full-back who'd been called up to make his first team debut.

That young man was Frank Yallop, who later went on to captain the club, play 389 times for them, and also represented Canada a lot. I'm sure he never forgot the car journey.

ZETA-JONES, Catherine

Came to the US Grand Prix at Indianapolis with her husband

Michael Douglas, and was immediately on my radar.

I remember asking her about Welsh racing drivers, and she was very chatty, as was Michael. Close up, she's a very attractive woman, but she never answers my calls!